SELECTIONS FROM THE PRINCIPLES OF PHILOSOPHY

OF

RENE DESCARTES (1596-1650)

TRANSLATED BY JOHN VEITCH, LL. D. LATE PROFESSOR OF
LOGIC AND RHETORIC IN THE UNIVERSITY OF GLASGOW

1901

This book has been published by:

Contact: sales@nuvisionpublications.com

URL: http://www.nuvisionpublications.com

Publishing Date: 2008

ISBN# 1-59547-686-5

Please see our website for several books created for
education, research and entertainment.

Specializing in rare, out-of-print books still in demand.

NuVision Publications, LLC is dedicated to bringing new life to rare, historic, and formerly out-of-print books. Most re-print publishers simply photocopy, or scan and print the pages from the original book, which can make the book hard to read as most re-print books are 100+ years old. It is our policy to take the time to convert the original faded, sometimes blotched text into crisp, clear digital text. All of our printed books have been completely reformatted to be easy to read and enjoy.

Please note that we do not correct out-of-date facts or grammar-type errors that were in the original book. We do our best to retain the original composition of the text, the way the author intended it.

NuVision Publications, LLC
Sioux Falls, SD USA

Contents

LETTER OF THE AUTHOR

TO THE FRENCH TRANSLATOR OF THE PRINCIPLES OF PHILOSOPHY SERVING FOR A PREFACE.

Sir,--The version of my principles which you have been at pains to make, is so elegant and finished as to lead me to expect that the work will be more generally read in French than in Latin, and better understood. The only apprehension I entertain is lest the title should deter some who have not been brought up to letters, or with whom philosophy is in bad repute, because the kind they were taught has proved unsatisfactory; and this makes me think that it will be useful to add a preface to it for the purpose of showing what the MATTER of the work is, what END I had in view in writing it, and what UTILITY may be derived from it. But although it might be my part to write a preface of this nature, seeing I ought to know those particulars better than any other person, I cannot nevertheless prevail upon myself to do anything more than merely to give a summary of the chief points that fall, as I think, to be discussed in it: and I leave it to your discretion to present to the public such part of them as you shall judge proper.

I should have desired, in the first place, to explain in it what philosophy is, by commencing with the most common matters, as, for example, that the word PHILOSOPHY signifies the study of wisdom, and that by wisdom is to be understood not merely prudence in the management of affairs, but a perfect knowledge of all that man can know, as well for the conduct of his life as for the preservation of his health and the discovery of all the arts, and that knowledge to subserve these ends must necessarily be deduced from first causes; so that in order to study the acquisition of it (which is properly called philosophizing), we must commence with the investigation of those first causes which are called PRINCIPLES. Now these principles must possess TWO CONDITIONS: in the first place, they must be so clear and evident that the human mind, when it attentively considers them, cannot doubt of their truth; in the second place, the knowledge of other things must be so dependent on them as that though the principles themselves may indeed be known apart from what depends on them, the latter cannot nevertheless be known apart from the former. It will accordingly be necessary thereafter to endeavour so to deduce from those principles the knowledge of the things that depend on them, as that there may be nothing in the whole series of deductions which is not perfectly manifest. God is in truth the only being who is absolutely wise, that is, who possesses a perfect knowledge of all things; but we may say that men are more or less wise as their knowledge of the most important truths is greater or less. And I am confident that there is nothing, in what I have now said, in which all the learned do not concur.

I should, in the next place, have proposed to consider the utility of philosophy, and at the same time have shown that, since it embraces all that the human mind can know, we ought to believe that it is by it we are distinguished from savages and barbarians, and that the civilisation and culture of a nation is regulated by the degree in which true philosophy nourishes in it, and, accordingly, that to contain true philosophers is the highest privilege a state can enjoy. Besides this, I should have shown that, as regards individuals, it is not only useful for each man to have intercourse with those who apply themselves to this study, but that it is incomparably better he should himself direct his attention to it; just as it is doubtless to be preferred that a man should make use of his own eyes to direct his steps, and enjoy by means of the same the beauties of colour and light, than that he should blindly follow the guidance of another; though the latter course is certainly better than to have the eyes closed with no guide except one's self. But to live without philosophizing is in truth the same as keeping the eyes closed without attempting to open them; and the pleasure of seeing all that sight discloses is not to be compared with the satisfaction afforded by the discoveries of philosophy. And, finally, this study is more imperatively requisite for the regulation of our manners, and for conducting us through life, than is the use of our eyes for directing our steps. The brutes, which have only their bodies to conserve, are continually occupied in seeking sources of nourishment; but men, of whom the chief part is the mind, ought to make the search after wisdom their principal care, for wisdom is the true nourishment of the mind; and I feel assured, moreover, that there are very many who would not fail in the search, if they would but hope for success in it, and knew the degree of their capabilities for it. There is no mind, how ignoble soever it be, which remains so firmly bound up in the objects of the senses, as not sometime or other to turn itself away from them in the aspiration after some higher good, although not knowing frequently wherein that good consists. The greatest favourites of fortune--those who have health, honours, and riches in abundance-- are not more exempt from aspirations of this nature than others; nay, I am persuaded that these are the persons who sigh the most deeply after another good greater and more perfect still than any they already possess. But the supreme good, considered by natural reason without the light of faith, is nothing more than the knowledge of truth through its first causes, in other words, the wisdom of which philosophy is the study. And, as all these particulars are indisputably true, all that is required to gain assent to their truth is that they be well stated.

But as one is restrained from assenting to these doctrines by experience, which shows that they who make pretensions to philosophy are often less wise and reasonable than others who never applied themselves to the study, I should have here shortly explained wherein consists all the science we now possess, and what are the degrees of wisdom at which we have arrived. The first degree contains only notions so clear of themselves that they can be acquired without meditation; the second comprehends all that the experience of the senses dictates; the third, that which the conversation of other men teaches us; to which may be added as the fourth, the reading, not of all books, but especially of such as have been written by persons capable of conveying proper instruction, for it is a species of conversation we hold with their authors. And it seems to me that all the wisdom we in ordinary possess is acquired only in these four ways; for I do not class divine revelation among them, because it does not conduct us by degrees, but elevates us at once to an infallible faith.

There have been, indeed, in all ages great minds who endeavoured to find a fifth road to wisdom, incomparably more sure and elevated than the other four. The path they essayed was the search of first causes and true principles, from which might be deduced the reasons of all that can be known by man; and it is to them the appellation of philosophers has been more especially accorded. I am not aware that there is any one of them up to the present who has succeeded in this enterprise. The first and chief whose writings we possess are Plato and Aristotle, between whom there was no difference, except that the former, following in the footsteps of his master, Socrates, ingenuously confessed that he had never yet been able to find anything certain, and that he was contented to write what seemed to him probable, imagining, for this end, certain principles by which he endeavoured to account for the other things. Aristotle, on the other hand, characterised by less candour, although for twenty years the disciple of Plato, and with no principles beyond those of his master, completely reversed his mode of putting them, and proposed as true and certain what it is probable he himself never esteemed as such. But these two men had acquired much judgment and wisdom by the four preceding means, qualities which raised their authority very high, so much so that those who succeeded them were willing rather to acquiesce in their opinions, than to seek better for themselves. The chief question among their disciples, however, was as to whether we ought to doubt of all things or hold some as certain,--a dispute which led them on both sides into extravagant errors; for a part of those who were for doubt, extended it even to the actions of life, to the neglect of the most ordinary rules required for its conduct; those, on the other hand, who maintained the doctrine of certainty, supposing that it must depend upon the senses, trusted entirely to them. To such an extent was this carried by Epicurus, that it is said he ventured to affirm, contrary to all the reasonings of the astronomers, that the sun is no larger than it appears.

It is a fault we may remark in most disputes, that, as truth is the mean between the two opinions that are upheld, each disputant departs from it in proportion to the degree in which he possesses the spirit of contradiction. But the error of those who leant too much to the side of doubt, was not followed for any length of time, and that of the opposite party has been to some extent corrected by the doctrine that the senses are deceitful in many instances. Nevertheless, I do not know that this error was wholly removed by showing that certitude is not in the senses, but in the understanding alone when it has clear perceptions; and that while we only possess the knowledge which is acquired in the first four grades of wisdom, we ought not to doubt of the things that appear to be true in what regards the conduct of life, nor esteem them as so certain that we cannot change our opinions regarding them, even though constrained by the evidence of reason.

From ignorance of this truth, or, if there was any one to whom it was known, from neglect of it, the majority of those who in these later ages aspired to be philosophers, blindly followed Aristotle, so that they frequently corrupted the sense of his writings, and attributed to him various opinions which he would not recognise as his own were he now to return to the world; and those who did not follow him, among whom are to be found many of the greatest minds, did yet not escape being imbued with his opinions in their youth, as these form the staple of instruction in the schools; and thus their minds were so preoccupied that they could not rise to the knowledge of true principles. And though I hold all the philosophers in esteem, and am unwilling to incur odium by my censure, I can adduce a proof of my assertion, which I do not think any of them will gainsay, which is, that they all laid down as a principle what they did not perfectly know. For example, I know none of them who did not suppose that there was gravity in terrestrial bodies; but although experience shows us very clearly that bodies we call heavy descend towards the center of the earth, we do not, therefore, know the nature of gravity, that is, the cause or principle in virtue of which bodies descend, and we must derive our knowledge of it from some other source. The same may be said of a vacuum and atoms, of heat and cold, of dryness and humidity, and of salt, sulphur, and mercury, and the other things of this sort which some have adopted as their principles. But no conclusion deduced from a principle which is not clear can be evident, even although the deduction be formally valid; and hence it follows that no reasonings based on such principles could lead them to the certain knowledge of any one thing, nor consequently advance them one step in the search after wisdom. And if they did discover any truth, this was due to one or other of the four means above mentioned. Notwithstanding this, I am in no degree desirous to lessen the honour which each of them can justly claim; I am only constrained to say, for the consolation of those who have not given their attention to study, that just as in travelling, when we turn our back upon the place to which we were going, we recede the farther from it in proportion as we proceed in the new direction for a greater length of time and with greater speed, so that, though we may be afterwards brought back to the right way, we cannot nevertheless arrive at the destined place as soon as if we had not moved backwards at all; so in philosophy, when we make use of false principles, we depart the farther from the knowledge of truth and wisdom exactly in proportion to the care with which we cultivate them, and apply ourselves to the deduction of diverse consequences from them, thinking that we are philosophizing well, while we are only departing the farther from the truth; from which it must be inferred that they who have learned the least of all that has been hitherto distinguished by the name of philosophy are the most fitted for the apprehension of truth.

After making those matters clear, I should, in the next place, have desired to set forth the grounds for holding that the true principles by which we may reach that highest degree of wisdom wherein consists the sovereign good of human life, are those I have proposed in this work; and two considerations alone are sufficient to establish this--the first of which is, that these principles are very clear, and the second, that we can deduce all other truths from them; for it is only these two conditions that are required in true principles. But I easily prove that they are very clear; firstly, by a reference to the manner in which I found them, namely, by rejecting all propositions that were in the least doubtful, for it is certain that such as could not be rejected by this test when they were attentively considered, are the most evident and clear which the human mind can know. Thus by considering that he who strives to doubt of all is unable nevertheless to doubt that he is while he doubts, and that what reasons thus, in not being able to doubt of itself and doubting nevertheless of everything else, is not that which we call our body, but what we name our mind or thought, I have taken the existence of this thought for the first principle, from which I very clearly deduced the following truths, namely, that there is a God who is the author of all that is in the world, and who, being the source of all truth, cannot have created our understanding of such a nature as to be deceived in the judgments it forms of the things of which it possesses a very clear and distinct perception. Those are all the principles of which I avail myself touching immaterial or metaphysical objects, from which I most clearly deduce these other principles of physical or corporeal things, namely, that there are bodies extended in length, breadth, and depth, which are of diverse figures and are moved in a variety of ways. Such are in sum the principles from which I deduce all other truths. The second circumstance that proves the clearness of these principles is, that they have been known in all ages, and even received as true and indubitable by all men, with the exception only of the existence of God, which has been doubted by some, because they attributed too much to the perceptions of the senses, and God can neither be seen nor touched.

But, though all the truths which I class among my principles were known at all times, and by all men, nevertheless, there has been no one up to the present, who, so far as I know, has adopted them as principles of philosophy: in other words, as such that we can deduce from them the knowledge of whatever else is in the world. It accordingly now remains for me to prove that they are such; and it appears to me that I cannot better establish this than by the test of experience: in other words, by inviting readers to peruse the following work. For, though I have not treated in it of all matters- -that being impossible--I think I have so explained all of which I had occasion to treat, that they who read it attentively will have ground for the persuasion that it is unnecessary to seek for any other principles than those I have given, in order to arrive at the most exalted knowledge of which the mind of man is capable; especially if, after the perusal of my writings, they take the trouble to consider how many diverse questions are therein discussed and explained, and, referring to the writings of others, they see how little probability there is in the reasons that are adduced in explanation of the same questions by principles different from mine. And that they may the more easily undertake this, I might have said that those imbued with my doctrines have much less difficulty in comprehending the writings of others, and estimating their true value, than those who have not been so imbued; and this is precisely the opposite of what I before said of such as commenced with the ancient philosophy, namely, that the more they have studied it the less fit are they for rightly apprehending the truth.

I should also have added a word of advice regarding the manner of reading this work, which is, that I should wish the reader at first to go over the whole of it, as he would a romance, without greatly straining his attention, or tarrying at the difficulties he may perhaps meet with in it, with the view simply of knowing in general the matters of which I treat; and that afterwards, if they seem to him to merit a more careful examination, and he feel a desire to know their causes, he may read it a second time, in order to observe the connection of my reasonings; but that he must not then give it up in despair, although he may not everywhere sufficiently discover the connection of the proof, or understand all the reasonings--it being only necessary to mark with a pen the places where the difficulties occur, and continue to read without interruption to the end; then, if he does not grudge to take up the book a third time, I am confident he will find in a fresh perusal the solution of most of the difficulties he will have marked before; and that, if any still remain, their solution will in the end be found in another reading.

I have observed, on examining the natural constitutions of different minds, that there are hardly any so dull or slow of understanding as to be incapable of apprehending good opinions, or even of acquiring all the highest sciences, if they be but conducted along the right road. And this can also be proved by reason; for, as the principles are clear, and as nothing ought to be deduced from them, unless most manifest inferences, no one is so devoid of intelligence as to be unable to comprehend the conclusions that flow from them. But, besides the entanglement of prejudices, from which no one is entirely exempt, although it is they who have been the most ardent students of the false sciences that receive the greatest detriment from them, it happens very generally that people of ordinary capacity neglect to study from a conviction that they want ability, and that others, who are more ardent, press on too rapidly: whence it comes to pass that they frequently admit principles far from evident, and draw doubtful inferences from them. For this reason, I should wish to assure those who are too distrustful of their own ability that there is nothing in my writings which they may not entirely understand, if they only take the trouble to examine them; and I should wish, at the same time, to warn those of an opposite tendency that even the most superior minds will have need of much time and attention to remark all I designed to embrace therein.

After this, that I might lead men to understand the real design I had in publishing them, I should have wished here to explain the order which it seems to me one ought to follow with the view of instructing himself. In the first place, a man who has merely the vulgar and imperfect knowledge which can be acquired by the four means above explained, ought, before all else, to endeavour to form for himself a code of morals, sufficient to regulate the actions of his life, as well for the reason that this does not admit of delay as because it ought to be our first care to live well. In the next place, he ought to study Logic, not that of the schools, for it is only, properly speaking, a dialectic which teaches the mode of expounding to others what we already know, or even of speaking much, without judgment, of what we do not know, by which means it corrupts rather than increases good sense--but the logic which teaches the right conduct of the reason with the view of discovering the truths of which we are ignorant; and, because it greatly depends on usage, it is desirable he should exercise himself for a length of time in practicing its rules on easy and simple questions, as those of the mathematics. Then, when he has acquired some skill in discovering the truth in these questions, he should commence to apply himself in earnest to true philosophy, of which the first part is Metaphysics, containing the principles of knowledge, among which is the explication of the principal attributes of God, of the immateriality of the soul, and of all the clear and simple notions that are in us; the second is Physics, in which, after finding the true principles of material things, we examine, in general, how the whole universe has been framed; in the next place, we consider, in particular, the nature of the earth, and of all the bodies that are most generally found upon it, as air, water, fire, the loadstone and other minerals. In the next place it is necessary also to examine singly the nature of plants, of animals, and above all of man, in order that we may thereafter be able to discover the other sciences that are useful to us. Thus, all Philosophy is like a tree, of which Metaphysics is the root, Physics the trunk, and all the other sciences the branches that grow out of this trunk, which are reduced to three principal, namely, Medicine, Mechanics, and Ethics. By the science of Morals, I understand the highest and most perfect which, presupposing an entire knowledge of the other sciences, is the last degree of wisdom.

But as it is not from the roots or the trunks of trees that we gather the fruit, but only from the extremities of their branches, so the principal utility of philosophy depends on the separate uses of its parts, which we can only learn last of all. But, though I am ignorant of almost all these, the zeal I have always felt in endeavouring to be of service to the public, was the reason why I published, some ten or twelve years ago, certain Essays on the doctrines I thought I had acquired. The first part of these Essays was a "Discourse on the Method of rightly conducting the Reason, and seeking Truth in the Sciences," in which I gave a summary of the principal rules of logic, and also of an imperfect ethic, which a person may follow provisionally so long as he does not know any better. The other parts were three treatises: the first of Dioptrics, the second of Meteors, and the third of Geometry. In the Dioptrics, I designed to show that we might proceed far enough in philosophy as to arrive, by its means, at the knowledge of the arts that are useful to life, because the invention of the telescope, of which I there gave an explanation, is one of the most difficult that has ever been made. In the treatise of Meteors, I desired to exhibit the difference that subsists between the philosophy I cultivate and that taught in the schools, in which the same matters are usually discussed. In fine, in the Geometry, I professed to demonstrate that I had discovered many things that were before unknown, and thus afford ground for believing that we may still discover many others, with the view of thus stimulating all to the investigation of truth. Since that period, anticipating the difficulty which many would experience in apprehending the foundations of the Metaphysics, I endeavoured to explain the chief points of them in a book of Meditations, which is not in itself large, but the size of which has been increased, and the matter greatly illustrated, by the Objections which several very learned persons sent to me on occasion of it, and by the Replies which I made to them. At length, after it appeared to me that those preceding treatises had sufficiently prepared the minds of my readers for the Principles of Philosophy, I also published it; and I have divided this work into four parts, the first of which contains the principles of human knowledge, and which may be called the First Philosophy, or Metaphysics. That this part, accordingly, may be properly understood, it will be necessary to read beforehand the book of Meditations I wrote on the same subject. The other three parts contain all that is most general in Physics, namely, the explication of the first laws or principles of nature, and the way in which the heavens, the fixed stars, the planets, comets, and generally the whole universe, were composed; in the next place, the explication, in particular, of the nature of this earth, the air, water, fire, the magnet, which are the bodies we most commonly find everywhere around it, and of all the qualities we observe in these bodies, as light, heat, gravity, and the like. In this way, it seems to me, I have commenced the orderly explanation of the whole of philosophy, without omitting any of the matters that ought to precede the last which I discussed. But to bring this undertaking to its conclusion, I ought hereafter to explain, in the same manner, the nature of the other more particular bodies that are on the earth, namely, minerals, plants, animals, and especially man; finally, to treat thereafter with accuracy of Medicine, Ethics, and Mechanics. I should require to do this in order to give to the world a complete body of philosophy; and I do not yet feel myself so old,- -I do not so much distrust my strength, nor do I find myself so far removed from the knowledge of what remains, as that I should not dare to undertake to complete this design, provided I were in a position to make all the experiments which I should require for the basis and verification of my reasonings. But seeing that would demand a great expenditure, to which the resources of a private individual like myself would not be adequate, unless aided by the public, and as I have no ground to expect this aid, I believe that I ought for the future to content myself with studying for my own instruction, and posterity will excuse me if I fail hereafter to labour for them.

Meanwhile, that it may be seen wherein I think I have already promoted the general good, I will here mention the fruits that may be gathered from my Principles. The first is the satisfaction which the mind will experience on finding in the work many truths before unknown; for although frequently truth does not so greatly affect our imagination as falsity and fiction, because it seems less wonderful and is more simple, yet the gratification it affords is always more durable and solid. The second fruit is, that in studying these principles we will become accustomed by degrees to judge better of all the things we come in contact with, and thus be made wiser, in which respect the effect will be quite the opposite of the common philosophy, for we may easily remark in those we call pedants that it renders them less capable of rightly exercising their reason than they would have been if they had never known it. The third is, that the truths which they contain, being highly clear and certain, will take away all ground of dispute, and thus dispose men's minds to gentleness and concord; whereas the contrary is the effect of the controversies of the schools, which, as they insensibly render those who are exercised in them more wrangling and opinionative, are perhaps the prime cause of the heresies and dissensions that now harass the world. The last and chief fruit of these Principles is, that one will be able, by cultivating them, to discover many truths I myself have not unfolded, and thus passing by degrees from one to another, to acquire in course of time a perfect knowledge of the whole of philosophy, and to rise to the highest degree of wisdom. For just as all the arts, though in their beginnings they are rude and imperfect, are yet gradually perfected by practice, from their containing at first something true, and whose effect experience evinces; so in philosophy, when we have true principles, we cannot fail by following them to meet sometimes with other truths; and we could not better prove the falsity of those of Aristotle, than by saying that men made no progress in knowledge by their means during the many ages they prosecuted them.

I well know that there are some men so precipitate and accustomed to use so little circumspection in what they do, that, even with the most solid foundations, they could not rear a firm superstructure; and as it is usually those who are the readiest to make books, they would in a short time mar all that I have done, and introduce uncertainty and doubt into my manner of philosophizing, from which I have carefully endeavoured to banish them, if people were to receive their writings as mine, or as representing my opinions. I had, not long ago, some experience of this in one of those who were believed desirous of following me the most closely,[1] and one too of whom I had somewhere said that I had such confidence in his genius as to believe that he adhered to no opinions which I should not be ready to avow as mine; for he last year published a book entitled "Fundamental Physics," in which, although he seems to have written nothing on the subject of Physics and Medicine which he did not take from my writings, as well from those I have published as from another still imperfect on the nature of animals, which fell into his hands; nevertheless, because he has copied them badly, and changed the order, and denied certain metaphysical truths upon which all Physics ought to be based, I am obliged wholly to disavow his work, and here to request readers not to attribute to me any opinion unless they find it expressly stated in my own writings, and to receive no opinion as true, whether in my writings or elsewhere, unless they see that it is very clearly deduced from true principles. I well know, likewise, that many ages may elapse ere all the truths deducible from these principles are evolved out of them, as well because the greater number of such as remain to be discovered depend on certain particular experiments that never occur by chance, but which require to be investigated with care and expense by men of the highest intelligence, as because it will hardly happen that the same persons who have the sagacity to make a right use of them, will possess also the means of making them, and also because the majority of the best minds have formed so low an estimate of philosophy in general, from the imperfections they have remarked in the kind in vogue up to the present time, that they cannot apply themselves to the search after truth.

But, in conclusion, if the difference discernible between the principles in question and those of every other system, and the great array of truths deducible from them, lead them to discern the importance of continuing the search after these truths, and to observe the degree of wisdom, the perfection and felicity of life, to which they are fitted to conduct us, I venture to believe that there will not be found one who is not ready to labour hard in so profitable a study, or at least to favour and aid with all his might those who shall devote themselves to it with success.

The height of my wishes is, that posterity may sometime behold the happy issue of it, etc.

---

[1] Regius; see La Vie de M. Descartes, reduite en abrege (Baillet). Liv. vii., chap. vii.--T.

TO THE MOST SERENE PRINCESS,

ELIZABETH, ELDEST DAUGHTER OF FREDERICK, KING OF BOHEMIA, COUNT PALATINE, AND ELECTOR OF THE SACRED ROMAN EMPIRE.

MADAM,--The greatest advantage I have derived from the writings which I have already published, has arisen from my having, through means of them, become known to your Highness, and thus been privileged to hold occasional converse with one in whom so many rare and estimable qualities are united, as to lead me to believe I should do service to the public by proposing them as an example to posterity. It would ill become me to flatter, or to give expression to anything of which I had no certain knowledge, especially in the first pages of a work in which I aim at laying down the principles of truth. And the generous modesty that is conspicuous in all your actions, assures me that the frank and simple judgment of a man who only writes what he believes will be more agreeable to you than the ornate laudations of those who have studied the art of compliment. For this reason, I will give insertion to nothing in this letter for which I have not the certainty both of experience and reason; and in the exordium, as in the rest of the work, I will write only as becomes a philosopher. There is a vast difference between real and apparent virtues; and there is also a great discrepancy between those real virtues that proceed from an accurate knowledge of the truth, and such as are accompanied with ignorance or error. The virtues I call apparent are only, properly speaking, vices, which, as they are less frequent than the vices that are opposed to them, and are farther removed from them than the intermediate virtues, are usually held in higher esteem than those virtues. Thus, because those who fear dangers too much are more numerous than they who fear them too little, temerity is frequently opposed to the vice of timidity, and taken for a virtue, and is commonly more highly esteemed than true fortitude. Thus, also, the prodigal are in ordinary more praised than the liberal; and none more easily acquire a great reputation for piety than the superstitious and hypocritical. With regard to true virtues, these do not all proceed from true knowledge, for there are some that likewise spring from defect or error; thus, simplicity is frequently the source of goodness, fear of devotion, and despair of courage. The virtues that are thus accompanied with some imperfections differ from each other, and have received diverse appellations. But those pure and perfect virtues that arise from the knowledge of good alone are all of the same nature, and may be comprised under the single term wisdom. For, whoever

17

owns the firm and constant resolution of always using his reason as well as lies in his power, and in all his actions of doing what he judges to be best, is truly wise, as far as his nature permits; and by this alone he is just, courageous, temperate, and possesses all the other virtues, but so well balanced as that none of them appears more prominent than another: and for this reason, although they are much more perfect than the virtues that blaze forth through the mixture of some defect, yet, because the crowd thus observes them less, they are not usually extolled so highly. Besides, of the two things that are requisite for the wisdom thus described, namely, the perception of the understanding and the disposition of the will, it is only that which lies in the will which all men can possess equally, inasmuch as the understanding of some is inferior to that of others. But although those who have only an inferior understanding may be as perfectly wise as their nature permits, and may render themselves highly acceptable to God by their virtue, provided they preserve always a firm and constant resolution to do all that they shall judge to be right, and to omit nothing that may lead them to the knowledge of the duties of which they are ignorant; nevertheless, those who preserve a constant resolution of performing the right, and are especially careful in instructing themselves, and who possess also a highly perspicacious intellect, arrive doubtless at a higher degree of wisdom than others; and I see that these three particulars are found in great perfection in your Highness. For, in the first place, your desire of self-instruction is manifest, from the circumstance that neither the amusements of the court, nor the accustomed mode of educating ladies, which ordinarily condemns them to ignorance, have been sufficient to prevent you from studying with much care all that is best in the arts and sciences; and the incomparable perspicacity of your intellect is evinced by this, that you penetrated the secrets of the sciences and acquired an accurate knowledge of them in a very short period. But of the vigour of your intellect I have a still stronger proof, and one peculiar to myself, in that I have never yet met any one who understood so generally and so well as yourself all that is contained in my writings. For there are several, even among men of the highest intellect and learning, who find them very obscure. And I remark, in almost all those who are versant in Metaphysics, that they are wholly disinclined from Geometry; and, on the other hand, that the cultivators of Geometry have no ability for the investigations of the First Philosophy: insomuch that I can say with truth I know but one mind, and that is your own, to which both studies are alike congenial, and which I therefore, with propriety, designate incomparable. But what most of all enhances my admiration is, that so accurate and varied an acquaintance with the whole circle of the sciences is not found in some aged doctor who has employed many years in contemplation, but in a Princess still young, and whose countenance and years would more fitly represent one of the Graces than a Muse or the sage Minerva. In conclusion, I not only remark in your Highness all that is requisite on the part of the mind to perfect and sublime wisdom, but also all that can be required on the part of the will or the manners, in which benignity and gentleness are so conjoined with majesty that, though fortune has attacked you with continued injustice, it has failed either to irritate or crush you. And this constrains me to such veneration that I not only think this work due to you, since it treats of philosophy which is the study of wisdom, but likewise feel not more zeal for my reputation as a philosopher than pleasure in subscribing myself,--

Of your most Serene Highness, The most devoted servant,

DESCARTES.

Part I

OF THE PRINCIPLES OF HUMAN KNOWLEDGE.

I. THAT in order to seek truth, it is necessary once in the course of our life, to doubt, as far as possible, of all things.

As we were at one time children, and as we formed various judgments regarding the objects presented to our senses, when as yet we had not the entire use of our reason, numerous prejudices stand in the way of our arriving at the knowledge of truth; and of these it seems impossible for us to rid ourselves, unless we undertake, once in our lifetime, to doubt of all those things in which we may discover even the smallest suspicion of uncertainty.

II. That we ought also to consider as false all that is doubtful.

Moreover, it will be useful likewise to esteem as false the things of which we shall be able to doubt, that we may with greater clearness discover what possesses most certainty and is the easiest to know.

III. That we ought not meanwhile to make use of doubt in the conduct of life.

In the meantime, it is to be observed that we are to avail ourselves of this general doubt only while engaged in the contemplation of truth. For, as far as concerns the conduct of life, we are very frequently obliged to follow opinions merely probable, or even sometimes, though of two courses of action we may not perceive more probability in the one than in the other, to choose one or other, seeing the opportunity of acting would not unfrequently pass away before we could free ourselves from our doubts.

IV. Why we may doubt of sensible things.

Accordingly, since we now only design to apply ourselves to the investigation of truth, we will doubt, first, whether of all the things that have ever fallen under our senses, or which we have ever imagined, any one really exist; in the first place, because we know by experience that the senses sometimes err, and it would be imprudent to trust too much to what has even once deceived us; secondly, because in dreams we perpetually seem to perceive or imagine innumerable objects which have no existence. And to one who has thus resolved upon a general doubt, there appear no marks by which he can with certainty distinguish sleep from the waking state.

V. Why we may also doubt of mathematical demonstrations.

We will also doubt of the other things we have before held as most certain, even of the demonstrations of mathematics, and of their principles which we have hitherto deemed self-evident; in the first place, because we have sometimes seen men fall into error in such matters, and admit as absolutely certain and self evident what to us appeared false, but chiefly because we have learnt that God who created us is all-powerful; for we do not yet know whether perhaps it was his will to create us so that we are always deceived, even in the things we think we know best: since this does not appear more impossible than our being occasionally deceived, which, however, as observation teaches us, is the case. And if we suppose that an all- powerful God is not the author of our being, and that we exist of ourselves or by some other means, still, the less powerful we suppose our author to be, the greater reason will we have for believing that we are not so perfect as that we may not be continually deceived.

VI. That we possess a free-will, by which we can withhold our assent from what is doubtful, and thus avoid error.

But meanwhile, whoever in the end may be the author of our being, and however powerful and deceitful he may be, we are nevertheless conscious of a freedom, by which we can refrain from admitting to a place in our belief aught that is not manifestly certain and undoubted, and thus guard against ever being deceived.

VII. That we cannot doubt of our existence while we doubt, and that this is the first knowledge we acquire when we philosophize in order.

While we thus reject all of which we can entertain the smallest doubt, and even imagine that it is false, we easily indeed suppose that there is neither God, nor sky, nor bodies, and that we ourselves even have neither hands nor feet, nor, finally, a body; but we cannot in the same way suppose that we are not while we doubt of the truth of these things; for there is a repugnance in conceiving that what thinks does not exist at the very time when it thinks. Accordingly, the knowledge, *I THINK, THEREFORE I AM*, is the first and most certain that occurs to one who philosophizes orderly.

VIII. That we hence discover the distinction between the mind and the body, or between a thinking and corporeal thing.

And this is the best mode of discovering the nature of the mind, and its distinctness from the body: for examining what we are, while supposing, as we now do, that there is nothing really existing apart from our thought, we clearly perceive that neither extension, nor figure, nor local motion,[2] nor anything similar that can be attributed to body, pertains to our nature, and nothing save thought alone; and, consequently, that the notion we have of our mind precedes that of any corporeal thing, and is more certain, seeing we still doubt whether there is any body in existence, while we already perceive that we think.

IX. What thought (COGITATIO) is.

By the word thought, I understand all that which so takes place in us that we of ourselves are immediately conscious of it; and, accordingly, not only to understand (INTELLIGERE, ENTENDRE), to will (VELLE), to imagine (IMAGINARI), but even to perceive (SENTIRE, SENTIR), are here the same as to think (COGITARE, PENSER). For if I say, I see, or, I walk, therefore I am; and if I understand by vision or walking the act of my eyes or of my limbs, which is the work of the body, the conclusion is not absolutely certain, because, as is often the case in dreams, I may think that I see or walk, although I do not open my eyes or move from my place, and even, perhaps, although I have no body: but, if I mean the sensation itself, or consciousness of seeing or walking, the knowledge is manifestly certain, because it is then referred to the mind, which alone perceives or is conscious that it sees or walks.[3]

X. That the notions which are simplest and self-evident, are obscured by logical definitions; and that such are not to be reckoned among the cognitions acquired by study, [but as born with us].

I do not here explain several other terms which I have used, or design to use in the sequel, because their meaning seems to me sufficiently self-evident. And I frequently remarked that philosophers erred in attempting to explain, by logical definitions, such truths as are most simple and self-evident; for they thus only rendered them more obscure. And when I said that the proposition, I THINK, THEREFORE I AM, is of all others the first and most certain which occurs to one philosophizing orderly, I did not therefore deny that it was necessary to know what thought, existence, and certitude are, and the truth that, in order to think it is necessary to be, and the like; but, because these are the most simple notions, and such as of themselves afford the knowledge of nothing existing, I did not judge it proper there to enumerate them.

XI. How we can know our mind more clearly than our body.

But now that it may be discerned how the knowledge we have of the mind not only precedes, and has greater certainty, but is even clearer,

---

[2] Instead of "local motion," the French has "existence in any place."

[3] In the French, "which alone has the power of perceiving, or of being conscious in any other way whatever."

than that we have of the body, it must be remarked, as a matter that is highly manifest by the natural light, that to nothing no affections or qualities belong; and, accordingly, that where we observe certain affections, there a thing or substance to which these pertain, is necessarily found. The same light also shows us that we know a thing or substance more clearly in proportion as we discover in it a greater number of qualities. Now, it is manifest that we remark a greater number of qualities in our mind than in any other thing; for there is no occasion on which we know anything whatever when we are not at the same time led with much greater certainty to the knowledge of our own mind. For example, if I judge that there is an earth because I touch or see it, on the same ground, and with still greater reason, I must be persuaded that my mind exists; for it may be, perhaps, that I think I touch the earth while there is one in existence; but it is not possible that I should so judge, and my mind which thus judges not exist; and the same holds good of whatever object is presented to our mind.

XII. How it happens that every one does not come equally to know this.

Those who have not philosophized in order have had other opinions on this subject, because they never distinguished with sufficient care the mind from the body. For, although they had no difficulty in believing that they themselves existed, and that they had a higher assurance of this than of any other thing, nevertheless, as they did not observe that by THEMSELVES, they ought here to understand their MINDS alone [when the question related to metaphysical certainty]; and since, on the contrary, they rather meant their bodies which they saw with their eyes, touched with their hands, and to which they erroneously attributed the faculty of perception, they were prevented from distinctly apprehending the nature of the mind.

XIII. In what sense the knowledge of other things depends upon the knowledge of God.

But when the mind, which thus knows itself but is still in doubt as to all other things, looks around on all sides, with a view to the farther extension of its knowledge, it first of all discovers within itself the ideas of many things; and while it simply contemplates them, and neither affirms nor denies that there is anything beyond itself corresponding to them, it is in no danger of erring. The mind also discovers certain common notions out of which it frames various demonstrations that carry conviction to such a degree as to render doubt of their truth impossible, so long as we give attention to them. For example, the mind has within itself ideas of numbers and figures, and it has likewise among its common notions the principle THAT IF EQUALS BE ADDED TO EQUALS THE WHOLES WILL BE EQUAL and the like; from which it is easy to demonstrate that the three angles of a triangle are equal to two right angles, etc. Now, so long as we attend to the premises from which this conclusion and others similar to it were deduced, we feel assured of their truth; but, as the mind cannot always think of these with attention, when it has the remembrance of a conclusion without recollecting the order of its deduction, and is uncertain whether the author of its being has created it of a nature that is liable to be deceived, even in what appears most evident, it perceives that there is just ground to distrust the truth of such conclusions, and that it cannot possess any certain knowledge until it has discovered its author.

XIV. That we may validly infer the existence of God from necessary existence being comprised in the concept we have of him.

When the mind afterwards reviews the different ideas that are in it, it discovers what is by far the chief among them--that of a Being omniscient, all-powerful, and absolutely perfect; and it observes that in this idea there is contained not only possible and contingent existence, as in the ideas of all other things which it clearly perceives, but existence absolutely necessary and eternal. And just as because, for example, the equality of its three angles to two right angles is necessarily comprised in the idea of a triangle, the mind is firmly persuaded that the three angles of a triangle are equal to two right angles; so, from its perceiving necessary and eternal existence to be comprised in the idea which it has of an all-perfect Being, it ought manifestly to conclude that this all-perfect Being exists.

XV. That necessary existence is not in the same way comprised in the notions which we have of other things, but merely contingent existence.

The mind will be still more certain of the truth of this conclusion, if it consider that it has no idea of any other thing in which it can discover that necessary existence is contained; for, from this circumstance alone, it will discern that the idea of an all-perfect Being has not been framed by itself, and that it does not represent a chimera, but a true and immutable nature, which must exist since it can only be conceived as necessarily existing.

XVI. That prejudices hinder many from clearly knowing the necessity of the existence of God.

Our mind would have no difficulty in assenting to this truth, if it were, first of all, wholly free from prejudices; but as we have been accustomed to distinguish, in all other things, essence from existence, and to imagine at will many ideas of things which neither are nor have been, it easily happens, when we do not steadily fix our thoughts on the contemplation of the all-perfect Being, that a doubt arises as to whether the idea we have of him is not one of those which we frame at pleasure, or at least of that class to whose essence existence does not pertain.

XVII. That the greater objective (representative) perfection there is in our idea of a thing, the greater also must be the perfection of its cause.

When we further reflect on the various ideas that are in us, it is easy to perceive that there is not much difference among them, when we consider them simply as certain modes of thinking, but that they are widely different, considered in reference to the objects they represent; and that their causes must be so much the more perfect according to the degree of objective perfection contained in them.[4] For there is no difference between this and the case of a person who has the idea of a machine, in the construction of which great skill is displayed, in which circumstances we have a right to inquire how he came by this idea, whether, for example, he somewhere saw such a machine constructed by another, or whether he was so accurately taught the mechanical sciences, or is endowed with such force of genius, that he was able of himself to invent it, without having elsewhere seen anything like it; for all the ingenuity which is contained in the idea objectively only, or as it were in a picture, must exist at least in its first and chief cause, whatever that may be, not only objectively or representatively, but in truth formally or eminently.

XVIII. That the existence of God may be again inferred from the above.

Thus, because we discover in our minds the idea of God, or of an all-perfect Being, we have a right to inquire into the source whence we derive it; and we will discover that the perfections it represents are so immense as to render it quite certain that we could only derive it from an all-perfect Being; that is, from a God really existing. For it is not only manifest by the natural light that nothing cannot be the cause of anything whatever, and that the more perfect cannot arise from the less perfect, so as to be thereby produced as by its efficient and total cause, but also that it is impossible we can have the idea or representation of anything whatever, unless there be somewhere, either in us or out of us, an original which comprises, in reality, all the perfections that are thus represented to us; but, as we do not in any way find in ourselves those absolute perfections of which we have the idea, we must conclude that they exist in some nature different from ours, that is, in God, or at least that they were once in him; and it most manifestly follows [from their infinity] that they are still there.

XIX. That, although we may not comprehend the nature of God, there is yet nothing which we know so clearly as his perfections.

This will appear sufficiently certain and manifest to those who have been accustomed to contemplate the idea of God, and to turn their thoughts to his infinite perfections; for, although we may not comprehend them, because it is of the nature of the infinite not to be comprehended by what is finite, we nevertheless conceive them more

---

[4] "as what they represent of their object has more perfection."--FRENCH.

clearly and distinctly than material objects, for this reason, that, being simple, and unobscured by limits,[5] they occupy our mind more fully.

XX. That we are not the cause of ourselves, but that this is God, and consequently that there is a God.

But, because every one has not observed this, and because, when we have an idea of any machine in which great skill is displayed, we usually know with sufficient accuracy the manner in which we obtained it, and as we cannot even recollect when the idea we have of a God was communicated to us by him, seeing it was always in our minds, it is still necessary that we should continue our review, and make inquiry after our author, possessing, as we do, the idea of the infinite perfections of a God: for it is in the highest degree evident by the natural light, that that which knows something more perfect than itself, is not the source of its own being, since it would thus have given to itself all the perfections which it knows; and that, consequently, it could draw its origin from no other being than from him who possesses in himself all those perfections, that is, from God.

XXI. That the duration alone of our life is sufficient to demonstrate the existence of God.

The truth of this demonstration will clearly appear, provided we consider the nature of time, or the duration of things; for this is of such a kind that its parts are not mutually dependent, and never co-existent; and, accordingly, from the fact that we now are, it does not necessarily follow that we shall be a moment afterwards, unless some cause, viz., that which first produced us, shall, as it were, continually reproduce us, that is, conserve us. For we easily understand that there is no power in us by which we can conserve ourselves, and that the being who has so much power as to conserve us out of himself, must also by so much the greater reason conserve himself, or rather stand in need of being conserved by no one whatever, and, in fine, be God.

XXII. That in knowing the existence of God, in the manner here explained, we likewise know all his attributes, as far as they can be known by the natural light alone.

There is the great advantage in proving the existence of God in this way, viz., by his idea, that we at the same time know what he is, as far as the weakness of our nature allows; for, reflecting on the idea we have of him which is born with us, we perceive that he is eternal, omniscient, omnipotent, the source of all goodness and truth, creator of all things, and that, in fine, he has in himself all that in which we can

---

[5] After LIMITS, "what of them we do conceive is much less confused. There is, besides, no speculation more calculated to aid in perfecting our understanding, and which is more important than this, inasmuch as the consideration of an object that has no limits to its perfections fills us with satisfaction and assurance."-FRENCH.

clearly discover any infinite perfection or good that is not limited by any imperfection.

XXIII. That God is not corporeal, and does not perceive by means of senses as we do, or will the evil of sin.

For there are indeed many things in the world that are to a certain extent imperfect or limited, though possessing also some perfection; and it is accordingly impossible that any such can be in God. Thus, looking to corporeal nature,[6] since divisibility is included in local extension, and this indicates imperfection, it is certain that God is not body. And although in men it is to some degree a perfection to be capable of perceiving by means of the senses, nevertheless since in every sense there is passivity [Footnote: In the French, "because our perceptions arise from impressions made upon us from another source," i.e., than ourselves.] which indicates dependency, we must conclude that God is in no manner possessed of senses, and that he only understands and wills, not, however, like us, by acts in any way distinct, but always by an act that is one, identical, and the simplest possible, understands, wills, and operates all, that is, all things that in reality exist; for he does not will the evil of sin, seeing this is but the negation of being.

XXIV. That in passing from the knowledge of God to the knowledge of the creatures, it is necessary to remember that our understanding is finite, and the power of God infinite.

But as we know that God alone is the true cause of all that is or can be, we will doubtless follow the best way of philosophizing, if, from the knowledge we have of God himself, we pass to the explication of the things which he has created, and essay to deduce it from the notions that are naturally in our minds, for we will thus obtain the most perfect science, that is, the knowledge of effects through their causes. But that we may be able to make this attempt with sufficient security from error, we must use the precaution to bear in mind as much as possible that God, who is the author of things, is infinite, while we are wholly finite.

XXV. That we must believe all that God has revealed, although it may surpass the reach of our faculties.

Thus, if perhaps God reveal to us or others, matters concerning himself which surpass the natural powers of our mind, such as the mysteries of the incarnation and of the trinity, we will not refuse to believe them, although we may not clearly understand them; nor will we be in any way surprised to find in the immensity of his nature, or even in what he has created, many things that exceed our comprehension.

---

[6] In the French, "since extension constitutes the nature of body."

XXVI. That it is not needful to enter into disputes[7] regarding the infinite, but merely to hold all that in which we can find no limits as indefinite, such as the extension of the world, the divisibility of the parts of matter, the number of the stars, etc.

We will thus never embarrass ourselves by disputes about the infinite, seeing it would be absurd for us who are finite to undertake to determine anything regarding it, and thus as it were to limit it by endeavouring to comprehend it. We will accordingly give ourselves no concern to reply to those who demand whether the half of an infinite line is also infinite, and whether an infinite number is even or odd, and the like, because it is only such as imagine their minds to be infinite who seem bound to entertain questions of this sort. And, for our part, looking to all those things in which in certain senses, we discover no limits, we will not, therefore, affirm that they are infinite, but will regard them simply as indefinite. Thus, because we cannot imagine extension so great that we cannot still conceive greater, we will say that the magnitude of possible things is indefinite, and because a body cannot be divided into parts so small that each of these may not be conceived as again divided into others still smaller, let us regard quantity as divisible into parts whose number is indefinite; and as we cannot imagine so many stars that it would seem impossible for God to create more, let us suppose that their number is indefinite, and so in other instances.

XXVII. What difference there is between the indefinite and the infinite.

And we will call those things indefinite rather than infinite, with the view of reserving to God alone the appellation of infinite; in the first place, because not only do we discover in him alone no limits on any side, but also because we positively conceive that he admits of none; and in the second place, because we do not in the same way positively conceive that other things are in every part unlimited, but merely negatively admit that their limits, if they have any, cannot be discovered by us.

XXVIII. That we must examine, not the final, but the efficient, causes of created things.

Likewise, finally, we will not seek reasons of natural things from the end which God or nature proposed to himself in their creation (i. e., final causes),[8] for we ought not to presume so far as to think that we are sharers in the counsels of Deity, but, considering him as the efficient cause of all things, let us endeavour to discover by the natural light[9] which he has planted in us, applied to those of his attributes of which he

---

[7] "to essay to comprehend the infinite."--FRENCH.
[8] "We will not stop to consider the ends which God proposed to himself in the creation of the world, and we will entirely reject from our philosophy the search of final causes!"--French.
[9] "Faculty of reasoning."—FRENCH.

has been willing we should have some knowledge, what must be concluded regarding those effects we perceive by our senses; bearing in mind, however, what has been already said, that we must only confide in this natural light so long as nothing contrary to its dictates is revealed by God himself.[10]

XXIX. That God is not the cause of our errors.

The first attribute of God which here falls to be considered, is that he is absolutely veracious and the source of all light, so that it is plainly repugnant for him to deceive us, or to be properly and positively the cause of the errors to which we are consciously subject; for although the address to deceive seems to be some mark of subtlety of mind among men, yet without doubt the will to deceive only proceeds from malice or from fear and weakness, and consequently cannot be attributed to God.

XXX. That consequently all which we clearly perceive is true, and that we are thus delivered from the doubts above proposed.

Whence it follows, that the light of nature, or faculty of knowledge given us by God, can never compass any object which is not true, in as far as it attains to a knowledge of it, that is, in as far as the object is clearly and distinctly apprehended. For God would have merited the appellation of a deceiver if he had given us this faculty perverted, and such as might lead us to take falsity for truth [when we used it aright]. Thus the highest doubt is removed, which arose from our ignorance on the point as to whether perhaps our nature was such that we might be deceived even in those things that appear to us the most evident. The same principle ought also to be of avail against all the other grounds of doubting that have been already enumerated. For mathematical truths ought now to be above suspicion, since these are of the clearest. And if we perceive anything by our senses, whether while awake or asleep, we will easily discover the truth provided we separate what there is of clear and distinct in the knowledge from what is obscure and confused. There is no need that I should here say more on this subject, since it has already received ample treatment in the metaphysical Meditations; and what follows will serve to explain it still more accurately.

XXXI. That our errors are, in respect of God, merely negations, but, in respect of ourselves, privations.

But as it happens that we frequently fall into error, although God is no deceiver, if we desire to inquire into the origin and cause of our errors, with a view to guard against them, it is necessary to observe that they depend less on our understanding than on our will, and that they have no need of the actual concourse of God, in order to their production; so that, when considered in reference to God, they are merely negations, but in reference to ourselves, privations.

---

[10] The last clause, beginning "bearing in mind." is omitted in the French.

XXXII. That there are only two modes of thinking in us, viz., the perception of the understanding and the action of the will.

For all the modes of thinking of which we are conscious may be referred to two general classes, the one of which is the perception or operation of the understanding, and the other the volition or operation of the will. Thus, to perceive by the senses (SENTIRE), to imagine, and to conceive things purely intelligible, are only different modes of perceiving (PERCIP IENDI); but to desire, to be averse from, to affirm, to deny, to doubt, are different modes of willing.

XXXIII. That we never err unless when we judge of something which we do not sufficiently apprehend.

When we apprehend anything we are in no danger of error, if we refrain from judging of it in any way; and even when we have formed a judgment regarding it, we would never fall into error, provided we gave our assent only to what we clearly and distinctly perceived; but the reason why we are usually deceived, is that we judge without possessing an exact knowledge of that of which we judge.

XXXIV. That the will as well as the understanding is required for judging.

I admit that the understanding is necessary for judging, there being no room to suppose that we can judge of that which we in no way apprehend; but the will also is required in order to our assenting to what we have in any degree perceived. It is not necessary, however, at least to form any judgment whatever, that we have an entire and perfect apprehension of a thing; for we may assent to many things of which we have only a very obscure and confused knowledge.

XXXV. That the will is of greater extension than the understanding, and is thus the source of our errors.

Further, the perception of the intellect extends only to the few things that are presented to it, and is always very limited: the will, on the other hand, may, in a certain sense, be said to be infinite, because we observe nothing that can be the object of the will of any other, even of the unlimited will of God, to which ours cannot also extend, so that we easily carry it beyond the objects we clearly perceive; and when we do this, it is not wonderful that we happen to be deceived.

XXXVI. That our errors cannot be imputed to God.

But although God has not given us an omniscient understanding, he is not on this account to be considered in any wise the author of our errors, for it is of the nature of created intellect to be finite, and of finite intellect not to embrace all things.

XXXVII. That the chief perfection of man is his being able to act freely or by will, and that it is this which renders him worthy of praise or blame.

That the will should be the more extensive is in harmony with its nature: and it is a high perfection in man to be able to act by means of it, that is, freely; and thus in a peculiar way to be the master of his own actions, and merit praise or blame. For self- acting machines are not commended because they perform with exactness all the movements for which they were adapted, seeing their motions are carried on necessarily; but the maker of them is praised on account of the exactness with which they were framed, because he did not act of necessity, but freely; and, on the same principle, we must attribute to ourselves something more on this account, that when we embrace truth, we do so not of necessity, but freely.

XXXVIII. That error is a defect in our mode of acting, not in our nature; and that the faults of their subjects may be frequently attributed to other masters, but never to God.

It is true, that as often as we err, there is some defect in our mode of action or in the use of our liberty, but not in our nature, because this is always the same, whether our judgments be true or false. And although God could have given to us such perspicacity of intellect that we should never have erred, we have, notwithstanding, no right to demand this of him; for, although with us he who was able to prevent evil and did not is held guilty of it, God is not in the same way to be reckoned responsible for our errors because he had the power to prevent them, inasmuch as the dominion which some men possess over others has been instituted for the purpose of enabling them to hinder those under them from doing evil, whereas the dominion which God exercises over the universe is perfectly absolute and free. For this reason we ought to thank him for the goods he has given us, and not complain that he has not blessed us with all which we know it was in his power to impart.

XXXIX. That the liberty of our will is self-evident.

Finally, it is so manifest that we possess a free will, capable of giving or withholding its assent, that this truth must be reckoned among the first and most common notions which are born with us. This, indeed, has already very clearly appeared, for when essaying to doubt of all things, we went so far as to suppose even that he who created us employed his limitless power in deceiving us in every way, we were conscious nevertheless of being free to abstain from believing what was not in every respect certain and undoubted. Bat that of which we are unable to doubt at such a time is as self- evident and clear as any thing we can ever know.

XL. That it is likewise certain that God has fore-ordained all things.

But because what we have already discovered of God, gives us the assurance that his power is so immense that we would sin in thinking ourselves capable of ever doing anything which he had not ordained beforehand, we should soon be embarrassed in great difficulties if we undertook to harmonise the pre-ordination of God with the freedom of our will, and endeavoured to comprehend both truths at once.

XLI. How the freedom of our will may be reconciled with the Divine pre-ordination.

But, in place of this, we will be free from these embarrassments if we recollect that our mind is limited, while the power of God, by which he not only knew from all eternity what is or can be, but also willed and pre-ordained it, is infinite. It thus happens that we possess sufficient intelligence to know clearly and distinctly that this power is in God, but not enough to comprehend how he leaves the free actions of men indeterminate} and, on the other hand, we have such consciousness of the liberty and indifference which exists in ourselves, that there is nothing we more clearly or perfectly comprehend: [so that the omnipotence of God ought not to keep us from believing it]. For it would be absurd to doubt of that of which we are fully conscious, and which we experience as existing in ourselves, because we do not comprehend another matter which, from its very nature, we know to be incomprehensible.

XLII. How, although we never will to err, it is nevertheless by our will that we do err.

But now since we know that all our errors depend upon our will, and as no one wishes to deceive himself, it may seem wonderful that there is any error in our judgments at all. It is necessary to remark, however, that there is a great difference between willing to be deceived, and willing to yield assent to opinions in which it happens that error is found. For though there is no one who expressly wishes to fall into error, we will yet hardly find any one who is not ready to assent to things in which, unknown to himself, error lurks; and it even frequently happens that it is the desire itself of following after truth that leads those not fully aware of the order in which it ought to be sought for, to pass judgment on matters of which they have no adequate knowledge, and thus to fall into error.

XLIII. That we shall never err if we give our assent only to what we clearly and distinctly perceive.

But it is certain we will never admit falsity for truth, so long as we judge only of that which we clearly and distinctly perceive; because, as God is no deceiver, the faculty of knowledge which he has given us cannot be fallacious, nor, for the same reason, the faculty of will, when we do not extend it beyond the objects we clearly know. And even although this truth could not be established by reasoning, the minds of all have been so impressed by nature as spontaneously to assent to whatever is clearly perceived, and to experience an impossibility to doubt of its truth.

XLIV. That we uniformly judge improperly when we assent to what we do not clearly perceive, although our judgment may chance to be true; and that it is frequently our memory which deceives us by leading us to believe that certain things were formerly sufficiently understood by us.

It is likewise certain that, when we approve of any reason which we do not apprehend, we are either deceived, or, if we stumble on the truth, it is only by chance, and thus we can never possess the assurance that we are not in error. I confess it seldom happens that we judge of a thing when we have observed we do not apprehend it, because it is a dictate of the natural light never to judge of what we do not know. But we most frequently err in this, that we presume upon a past knowledge of much to which we give our assent, as to something treasured up in the memory, and perfectly known to us; whereas, in truth, we have no such knowledge.

XLV. What constitutes clear and distinct perception.

There are indeed a great many persons who, through their whole lifetime, never perceive anything in a way necessary for judging of it properly; for the knowledge upon which we can establish a certain and indubitable judgment must be not only clear, but also, distinct. I call that clear which is present and manifest to the mind giving attention to it, just as we are said clearly to see objects when, being present to the eye looking on, they stimulate it with sufficient force. and it is disposed to regard them; but the distinct is that which is so precise and different from all other objects as to comprehend in itself only what is clear.[11]

XLVI. It is shown, from the example of pain, that a perception may be clear without being distinct, but that it cannot be distinct unless it is clear.

For example, when any one feels intense pain, the knowledge which he has of this pain is very clear, but it is not always distinct; for men usually confound it with the obscure judgment they form regarding its nature, and think that there is in the suffering part something similar to the sensation of pain of which they are alone conscious. And thus perception may be clear without being distinct, but it can never be distinct without likewise being clear.

---

[11] "what appears manifestly to him who considers it as he ought."-- FRENCH.

XLVII. That, to correct the prejudices of our early years, we must consider what is clear in each of our simple[12] notions.

And, indeed, in our early years, the mind was so immersed in the body, that, although it perceived many things with sufficient clearness, it yet knew nothing distinctly; and since even at that time we exercised our judgment in many matters, numerous prejudices were thus contracted, which, by the majority, are never afterwards laid aside. But that we may now be in a position to get rid of these, I will here briefly enumerate all the simple notions of which our thoughts are composed, and distinguish in each what is clear from what is obscure, or fitted to lead into error.

XLVIII. That all the objects of our knowledge are to be regarded either (1) as things or the affections of things: or (2) as eternal truths; with the enumeration of things.

Whatever objects fall under our knowledge we consider either as things or the affections of things,[13] or as eternal truths possessing no existence beyond our thought. Of the first class the most general are substance, duration, order, number, and perhaps also some others, which notions apply to all the kinds of things. I do not, however, recognise more than two highest kinds (SUMMA GENERA) of things; the first of intellectual things, or such as have the power of thinking, including mind or thinking substance and its properties; the second, of material things, embracing extended substance, or body and its properties. Perception, volition, and all modes as well of knowing as of willing, are related to thinking substance; on the other hand, to extended substance we refer magnitude, or extension in length, breadth, and depth, figure, motion, situation, divisibility of parts themselves, and the like. There are, however, besides these, certain things of which we have an internal experience that ought not to be referred either to the mind of itself, or to the body alone, but to the close and intimate union between them, as will hereafter be shown in its place. Of this class are the appetites of hunger and thirst, etc., and also the emotions or passions of the mind which are not exclusively mental affections, as the emotions of anger, joy, sadness, love, etc.; and, finally, all the sensations, as of pain, titillation, light and colours, sounds, smells, tastes, heat, hardness, and the other tactile qualities.

XLIX. That the eternal truths cannot be thus enumerated, but that this is not necessary.

What I have already enumerated we are to regard as things, or the qualities or modes of things. We now come to speak of eternal truths.

---

[12] "first."-- FRENCH.

[13] Things and the affections of things are (in the French) equivalent to "what has some (i.e., a REAL) existence," as opposed to the class of "eternal truths," which have merely an IDEAL existence.

When we apprehend that it is impossible a thing can arise from nothing, this proposition, EX NIHILO NIHIL FIT, is not considered as somewhat existing, or as the mode of a thing, but as an eternal truth having its seat in our mind, and is called a common notion or axiom. Of this class are the following:--It is impossible the same thing can at once be and not be; what is done cannot be undone; he who thinks must exist while he thinks; and innumerable others, the whole of which it is indeed difficult to enumerate, but this is not necessary, since, if blinded by no prejudices, we cannot fail to know them when the occasion of thinking them occurs.

L. That these truths are clearly perceived, but not equally by all men, on account of prejudices.

And, indeed, with regard to these common notions, it is not to be doubted that they can be clearly and distinctly known, for otherwise they would not merit this appellation: as, in truth, some of them are not, with respect to all men, equally deserving of the name, because they are not equally admitted by all: not, however, from this reason, as I think, that the faculty of knowledge of one man extends farther than that of another, but rather because these common notions are opposed to the prejudices of some, who, on this account, are not able readily to embrace them, even although others, who are free from those prejudices, apprehend them with the greatest clearness.

LI. What substance is, and that the term is not applicable to God and the creatures in the same sense.

But with regard to what we consider as things or the modes of things, it is worth while to examine each of them by itself. By substance we can conceive nothing else than a thing which exists in such a way as to stand in need of nothing beyond itself in order to its existence. And, in truth, there can be conceived but one substance which is absolutely independent, and that is God. We perceive that all other things can exist only by help of the concourse of God. And, accordingly, the term substance does not apply to God and the creatures UNIVOCALLY, to adopt a term familiar in the schools; that is, no signification of this word can be distinctly understood which is common to God and them.

LII. That the term is applicable univocally to the mind and the body, and how substance itself is known.

Created substances, however, whether corporeal or thinking, may be conceived under this common concept; for these are things which, in order to their existence, stand in need of nothing but the concourse of God. But yet substance cannot be first discovered merely from its being a thing which exists independently, for existence by itself is not observed by us. We easily, however, discover substance itself from any attribute of it, by this common notion, that of nothing there are no attributes, properties, or qualities: for, from perceiving that some attribute is present, we infer that some existing thing or substance to which it may be attributed is also of necessity present.

LIII. That of every substance there is one principal attribute, as thinking of the mind, extension of the body.

But, although any attribute is sufficient to lead us to the knowledge of substance, there is, however, one principal property of every substance, which constitutes its nature or essence, and upon which all the others depend. Thus, extension in length, breadth, and depth, constitutes the nature of corporeal substance; and thought the nature of thinking substance. For every other thing that can be attributed to body, presupposes extension, and is only some mode of an extended thing; as all the properties we discover in the mind are only diverse modes of thinking. Thus, for example, we cannot conceive figure unless in something extended, nor motion unless in extended space, nor imagination, sensation, or will, unless in a thinking thing. But, on the other hand, we can conceive extension without figure or motion, and thought without imagination or sensation, and so of the others; as is clear to any one who attends to these matters.

LIV. How we may have clear and distinct notions of the substance which thinks, of that which is corporeal, and of God.

And thus we may easily have two clear and distinct notions or ideas, the one of created substance, which thinks, the other of corporeal substance, provided we carefully distinguish all the attributes of thought from those of extension. We may also have a clear and distinct idea of an uncreated and independent thinking substance, that is, of God, provided we do not suppose that this idea adequately represents to us all that is in God, and do not mix up with it anything fictitious, but attend simply to the characters that are comprised in the notion we have of him, and which we clearly know to belong to the nature of an absolutely perfect Being. For no one can deny that there is in us such an idea of God, without groundlessly supposing that there is no knowledge of God at all in the human mind.

LV. How duration, order, and number may be also distinctly conceived.

We will also have most distinct conceptions of duration, order, and number, if, in place of mixing up with our notions of them that which properly belongs to the concept of substance, we merely think that the duration of a thing is a mode under which we conceive this thing, in so far as it continues to exist; and, in like manner, that order and number are not in reality different from things disposed in order and numbered, but only modes under which we diversely consider these things.

LVI. What are modes, qualities, attributes.

And, indeed, we here understand by modes the same with what we elsewhere designate attributes or qualities. But when we consider substance as affected or varied by them, we use the term modes; when from this variation it may be denominated of such a kind, we adopt the term qualities [to designate the different modes which cause it to be so named]; and, finally, when we simply regard these modes as in the substance, we call them attributes. Accordingly, since God must be conceived as superior to change, it is not proper to say that there are modes or qualities in him, but simply attributes; and even in created things that which is found in them always in the same mode, as existence and duration in the thing which exists and endures, ought to be called attribute and not mode or quality.

LVII. That some attributes exist in the things to which they are attributed, and others only in our thought; and what duration and time are.

Of these attributes or modes there are some which exist in the things themselves, and others that have only an existence in our thought; thus, for example, time, which we distinguish from duration taken in its generality, and call the measure of motion, is only a certain mode under which we think duration itself, for we do not indeed conceive the duration of things that are moved to be different from the duration of things that are not moved: as is evident from this, that if two bodies are in motion for an hour, the one moving quickly and the other slowly, we do not reckon more time in the one than in the other, although there may be much more motion in the one of the bodies than in the other. But that we may comprehend the duration of all things under a common measure, we compare their duration with that of the greatest and most regular motions that give rise to years and days, and which we call time; hence what is so designated is nothing superadded to duration, taken in its generality, but a mode of thinking.

LVIII. That number and all universals are only modes of thought.

In the same way number, when it is not considered as in created things, but merely in the abstract or in general, is only a mode of thinking; and the same is true of all those general ideas we call universals.

LIX. How universals are formed; and what are the five common, viz., genus, species, difference, property, and accident.

Universals arise merely from our making use of one and the same idea in thinking of all individual objects between which there subsists a certain likeness; and when we comprehend all the objects represented by this idea under one name, this term likewise becomes universal. For example, when we see two stones, and do not regard their nature farther than to remark that there are two of them, we form the idea of a certain number, which we call the binary; and when we afterwards see two birds or two trees, and merely take notice of them so far as to observe that there are two of them, we again take up the same idea as before, which is, accordingly, universal; and we likewise give to this number the same universal appellation of binary. In the same way, when we consider a figure of three sides, we form a certain idea, which we call the idea of a triangle, and we afterwards make use of it as the universal to represent to our mind all other figures of three sides. But when we remark more particularly that of figures of three sides, some have a right angle and others not, we form the universal idea of a right-angled triangle, which being related to the preceding as more general, may be called species; and the right angle the universal difference by which right-angled triangles are distinguished from all others; and farther, because the square of the side which sustains the right angle is equal to the squares of the other two sides, and because this property belongs only to this species of triangles, we may call it the universal property of the species. Finally, if we suppose that of these triangles some are moved and others not, this will be their universal accident; and, accordingly, we commonly reckon five universals, viz., genus, species, difference, property, accident.

LX. Of distinctions; and first of the real.

But number in things themselves arises from the distinction there is between them: and distinction is threefold, viz., real, modal, and of reason. The real properly subsists between two or more substances; and it is sufficient to assure us that two substances are really mutually distinct, if only we are able clearly and distinctly to conceive the one of them without the other. For the knowledge we have of God renders it certain that he can effect all that of which we have a distinct idea: wherefore, since we have now, for example, the idea of an extended and corporeal substance, though we as yet do not know with certainty whether any such thing is really existent, nevertheless, merely because we have the idea of it, we may be assured that such may exist; and, if it really exists, that every part which we can determine by thought must be really distinct from the other parts of the same substance. In the same way, since every one is conscious that he thinks, and that he in thought can exclude from himself every other substance, whether thinking or extended, it is certain that each of us thus considered is really distinct from every other thinking and corporeal substance. And although we suppose that God united a body to a soul so closely that it was impossible to form a more intimate union, and thus made a composite whole, the two substances would remain really distinct, notwithstanding this union; for with whatever tie God connected them, he was not able to rid himself of the power he possessed of separating them, or of conserving the one apart from the other, and the things which God can separate or conserve separately are really distinct.

LXI. Of the modal distinction.

There are two kinds of modal distinctions, viz., that between the mode properly so-called and the substance of which it is a mode, and that between two modes of the same substance. Of the former we have an example in this, that we can clearly apprehend substance apart from the mode which we say differs from it; while, on the other hand, we cannot conceive this mode without conceiving the substance itself. There is, for example, a modal distinction between figure or motion and corporeal substance in which both exist; there is a similar distinction between affirmation or recollection and the mind. Of the latter kind we have an illustration in our ability to recognise the one of two modes apart from the other, as figure apart from motion, and motion apart from figure; though we cannot think of either the one or the other without thinking of the common substance in which they adhere. If, for example, a stone is moved, and is withal square, we can, indeed, conceive its square figure without its motion, and reciprocally its motion without its square figure; but we can conceive neither this motion nor this figure apart from the substance of the stone. As for the distinction according to which the mode of one substance is different from another substance, or from the mode of another substance, as the motion of one body is different from another body or from the mind, or as motion is different from doubt, it seems to me that it should be called real rather than modal, because these modes cannot be clearly conceived apart from the really distinct substances of which they are the modes.

LXII. Of the distinction of reason (logical distinction).

Finally, the distinction of reason is that between a substance and some one of its attributes, without which it is impossible, however, we can have a distinct conception of the substance itself; or between two such attributes of a common substance, the one of which we essay to think without the other. This distinction is manifest from our inability to form a clear and distinct idea of such substance, if we separate from it such attribute; or to have a clear perception of the one of two such attributes if we separate it from the other. For example, because any substance which ceases to endure ceases also to exist, duration is not distinct from substance except in thought (RATIONE); and in general all the modes of thinking which we consider as in objects differ only in thought, as well from the objects of which they are thought as from each other in a common object.[14] It occurs, indeed, to me that I have elsewhere classed this kind of distinction with the modal (viz., towards the end of the Reply to the First Objections to the Meditations on the First Philosophy); but there it was only necessary to treat of these distinctions generally, and it was sufficient for my purpose at that time simply to distinguish both of them from the real.

---

[14] "and generally all the attributes that lead us to entertain different thoughts of the same thing, such as, for example, the extension of body and its property of divisibility, do not differ from the body which is to us the object of them, or from each other, unless as we sometimes confusedly think the one without thinking the other."--FRENCH.

LXIII. How thought and extension may be distinctly known, as constituting, the one the nature of mind, the other that of body.

Thought and extension may be regarded as constituting the natures of intelligent and corporeal substance; and then they must not be otherwise conceived than as the thinking and extended substances themselves, that is, as mind and body, which in this way are conceived with the greatest clearness and distinctness. Moreover, we more easily conceive extended or thinking substance than substance by itself, or with the omission of its thinking or extension. For there is some difficulty in abstracting the notion of substance from the notions of thinking and extension, which, in truth, are only diverse in thought itself (i.e., logically different); and a concept is not more distinct because it comprehends fewer properties, but because we accurately distinguish what is comprehended in it from all other notions.

LXIV. How these may likewise be distinctly conceived as modes of substance.

Thought and extension may be also considered as modes of substance; in as far, namely, as the same mind may have many different thoughts, and the same body, with its size unchanged, may be extended in several diverse ways, at one time more in length and less in breadth or depth, and at another time more in breadth and less in length; and then they are modally distinguished from substance, and can be conceived not less clearly and distinctly, provided they be not regarded as substances or things separated from others, but simply as modes of things. For by regarding them as in the substances of which they are the modes, we distinguish them from these substances, and take them for what in truth they are: whereas, on the other hand, if we wish to consider them apart from the substances in which they are, we should by this itself regard them as self-subsisting things, and thus confound the ideas of mode and substance.

LXV. How we may likewise know their modes.

In the same way we will best apprehend the diverse modes of thought, as intellection, imagination, recollection, volition, etc., and also the diverse modes of extension, or those that belong to extension, as all figures, the situation of parts and their motions, provided we consider them simply as modes of the things in which they are; and motion as far as it is concerned, provided we think merely of locomotion, without seeking to know the force that produces it, and which nevertheless I will essay to explain in its own place.

LXVI. How our sensations, affections, and appetites may be clearly known, although we are frequently wrong in our judgments regarding them.

There remain our sensations, affections, and appetites, of which we may also have a clear knowledge, if we take care to comprehend in the judgments we form of them only that which is precisely contained in our perception of them, and of which we are immediately conscious. There is, however, great difficulty in observing this, at least in respect of sensations; because we have all, without exception, from our youth judged that all the things we perceived by our senses had an existence beyond our thought, and that they were entirely similar to the sensations, that is, perceptions, we ad of them. Thus when, for example, we saw a certain colour, we thought we saw something occupying a place out of us, and which was entirely similar to that idea of colour we were then conscious of; and from the habit of judging in this way, we seemed to see this so clearly and distinctly that we esteemed it (i.e., the externality of the colour) certain and indubitable.

LXVII. That we are frequently deceived in our judgments regarding pain itself.

The same prejudice has place in all our other sensations, even in those of titillation and pain. For though we are not in the habit of believing that there exist out of us objects that resemble titillation and pain, we do not nevertheless consider these sensations as in the mind alone, or in our perception, but as in the hand, or foot, or some other part of our body. There is no reason, however, to constrain us to believe that the pain, for example, which we feel, as it were, in the foot is something out of the mind existing in the foot, or that the light which we see, as it were, in the sun exists in the sun as it is in us. Both these beliefs are prejudices of our early years, as will clearly appear in the sequel.

LXVIII. How in these things what we clearly conceive is to be distinguished from that in which we may be deceived.

But that we may distinguish what is clear in our sensations from what is obscure, we ought most carefully to observe that we possess a clear and distinct knowledge of pain, colour, and other things of this sort, when we consider them simply as sensations or thoughts; but that, when they are judged to be certain things subsisting beyond our mind, we are wholly unable to form any conception of them. Indeed, when any one tells us that he sees colour in a body or feels pain in one of his limbs, this is exactly the same as if he said that he there saw or felt something of the nature of which he was entirely ignorant, or that he did not know what he saw or felt. For although, when less attentively examining his thoughts, a person may easily persuade himself that he has some knowledge of it, since he supposes that there is something resembling that sensation of colour or of pain of which he is conscious; yet, if he reflects on what the sensation of colour or pain represents to him as existing in a coloured body or in a wounded member, he will find that of such he has absolutely no knowledge.

LXIX. That magnitude, figure, etc., are known far differently from colour, pain, etc.

What we have said above will be more manifest; especially if we consider that size in the body perceived, figure, motion (at least local, for philosophers by fancying other kinds of motion have rendered its nature less intelligible to themselves), the situation of parts, duration, number, and those other properties which, as we have already said, we clearly perceive in all bodies, are known by us in a way altogether different from that in which we know what colour is in the same body, or pain, smell, taste, or any other of those properties which I have said above must be referred to the senses. For although when we see a body we are not less assured of its existence from its appearing figured than from its appearing coloured,[15] we yet know with far greater clearness its property of figure than its colour.

LXX. That we may judge of sensible things in two ways, by the one of which we avoid error, by the other fall into it.

It is thus manifest that to say we perceive colours in objects is in reality equivalent to saying we perceive something in objects and are yet ignorant of what it is, except as that which determines in us a certain highly vivid and clear sensation, which we call the sensation of colours. There is, however, very great diversity in the manner of judging: for so long as we simply judge that there is an unknown something in objects (that is, in things such as they are, from which the sensation reached us), so far are we from falling into error that, on the contrary, we thus rather provide against it, for we are less apt to judge rashly of a thing which we observe we do not know. But when we think we perceive colours in objects, although we are in reality ignorant of what we then denominate colour, and are unable to conceive any resemblance between the colour we suppose to be in objects, and that of which we are conscious in sensation, yet because we do not observe this, or because there are in objects several properties, as size, figure, number, etc., which, as we clearly know, exist, or may exist in them as they are perceived by our senses or conceived by our understanding, we easily glide into the error of holding that what is called colour in objects is something entirely resembling the colour we perceive, and thereafter of supposing that we have a clear perception of what is in no way perceived by us.

LXXI. That the chief cause of our errors is to be found in the prejudices of our childhood.

And here we may notice the first and chief cause of our errors. In early life the mind was so closely bound to the body that it attended to nothing beyond the thoughts by which it perceived the objects that made impression on the body; nor as yet did it refer these thoughts to

_____

[15] "by the colour we perceive on occasion of it."-- FRENCH.

anything existing beyond itself, but simply felt pain when the body was hurt, or pleasure when anything beneficial to the body occurred, or if the body was so highly affected that it was neither greatly benefited nor hurt, the mind experienced the sensations we call tastes, smells, sounds, heat, cold, light, colours, and the like, which in truth are representative of nothing existing out of our mind, and which vary according to the diversities of the parts and modes in which the body is affected.[16] The mind at the same time also perceived magnitudes, figures, motions, and the like, which were not presented to it as sensations but as things or the modes of things existing, or at least capable of existing out of thought, although it did not yet observe this difference between these two kinds of perceptions. And afterwards when the machine of the body, which has been so fabricated by nature that it can of its own inherent power move itself in various ways, by turning itself at random on every side, followed after what was useful and avoided what was detrimental; the mind, which was closely connected with it, reflecting on the objects it pursued or avoided, remarked, for the first time, that they existed out of itself, and not only attributed to them magnitudes, figures, motions, and the like, which it apprehended either as things or as the modes of things, but, in addition, attributed to them tastes, odours, and the other ideas of that sort, the sensations of which were caused by itself;[17] and as it only considered other objects in so far as they were useful to the body, in which it was immersed, it judged that there was greater or less reality in each object, according as the impressions it caused on the body were more or less powerful. Hence arose the belief that there was more substance or body in rocks and metals than in air or water, because the mind perceived in them more hardness and weight. Moreover, the air was thought to be merely nothing so long as we experienced no agitation of it by the wind, or did not feel it hot or cold. And because the stars gave hardly more light than the slender flames of candles, we supposed that each star was but of this size. Again, since the mind did not observe that the earth moved on its axis, or that its superficies was curved like that of a globe, it was on that account more ready to judge the earth immovable and its surface flat. And our mind has been imbued from our infancy with a thousand other prejudices of the same sort which afterwards in our youth we forgot we had accepted without sufficient examination, and admitted as possessed of the highest truth and clearness, as if they had been known by means of our senses, or implanted in us by nature.

LXXII. That the second cause of our errors is that we cannot forget these prejudices.

And although now in our mature years, when the mind, being no longer wholly subject to the body, is not in the habit of referring all things to it, but also seeks to discover the truth of things considered in

---

[16] "which vary according to the diversities of the movements that pass from all parts of our body to the part of the brain to which it (the mind) is closely joined and united."--FRENCH.

[17] "which it perceived on occasion of them" (i.e., of external objects).--FRENCH.

44

themselves, we observe the falsehood of a great many of the judgments we had before formed; yet we experience a difficulty in expunging them from our memory, and, so long as they remain there, they give rise to various errors. Thus, for example, since from our earliest years we imagined the stars to be of very small size, we find it highly difficult to rid ourselves of this imagination, although assured by plain astronomical reasons that they are of the greatest,--so prevailing is the power of preconceived opinion.

LXXIII. The third cause is, that we become fatigued by attending to those objects which are not present to the senses; and that we are thus accustomed to judge of these not from present perception but from pre-conceived opinion.

Besides, our mind cannot attend to any object without at length experiencing some pain and fatigue; and of all objects it has the greatest difficulty in attending to those which are present neither to the senses nor to the imagination: whether for the reason that this is natural to it from its union with the body, or because in our early years, being occupied merely with perceptions and imaginations, it has become more familiar with, and acquired greater facility in thinking in those modes than in any other. Hence it also happens that many are unable to conceive any substance except what is imaginable and corporeal, and even sensible. For they are ignorant of the circumstance, that those objects alone are imaginable which consist in extension, motion, and figure, while there are many others besides these that are intelligible; and they persuade themselves that nothing can subsist but body, and, finally, that there is no body which is not sensible. And since in truth we perceive no object such as it is by sense alone [but only by our reason exercised upon sensible objects], as will hereafter be clearly shown, it thus happens that the majority during life perceive nothing unless in a confused way.

LXXIV. The fourth source of our errors is, that we attach our thoughts to words which do not express them with accuracy.

Finally, since for the use of speech we attach all our conceptions to words by which to express them, and commit to memory our thoughts in connection with these terms, and as we afterwards find it more easy to recall the words than the things signified by them, we can scarcely conceive anything with such distinctness as to separate entirely what we conceive from the words that were selected to express it. On this account the majority attend to words rather than to things; and thus very frequently assent to terms without attaching to them any meaning, either because they think they once understood them, or imagine they received them from others by whom they were correctly understood. This, however, is not the place to treat of this matter in detail, seeing the nature of the human body has not yet been expounded, nor the existence even of body established; enough, nevertheless, appears to have been said to enable one to distinguish such of our conceptions as are clear and distinct from those that are obscure and confused.

LXXV. Summary of what must be observed in order to philosophize correctly.

Wherefore if we would philosophize in earnest, and give ourselves to the search after all the truths we are capable of knowing, we must, in the first place, lay aside our prejudices; in other words, we must take care scrupulously to withhold our assent from the opinions we have formerly admitted, until upon new examination we discover that they are true. We must, in the next place, make an orderly review of the notions we have in our minds, and hold as true all and only those which we will clearly and distinctly apprehend. In this way we will observe, first of all, that we exist in so far as it is our nature to think, and at the same time that there is a God upon whom we depend; and after considering his attributes we will be able to investigate the truth of all other things, since God is the cause of them. Besides the notions we have of God and of our mind, we will likewise find that we possess the knowledge of many propositions which are eternally true, as, for example, that nothing cannot be the cause of anything, etc. We will farther discover in our minds the knowledge of a corporeal or extended nature that may be moved, divided, etc., and also of certain sensations that affect us, as of pain, colours, tastes, etc., although we do not yet know the cause of our being so affected; and, comparing what we have now learne'd, by examining those things in their order, with our former confused knowledge of them, we will acquire the habit of forming clear and distinct conceptions of all the objects we are capable of knowing. In these few precepts seem to me to be comprised the most general and important principles of human knowledge.

LXXVI. That we ought to prefer the Divine authority to our perception;[18] but that, apart from things revealed, we ought to assent to nothing that we do not clearly apprehend.

Above all, we must impress on our memory the infallible rule, that what God has revealed is incomparably more certain than anything else; and that, we ought to submit our belief to the Divine authority rather than to our own judgment, even although perhaps the light of reason should, with the greatest clearness and evidence, appear to suggest to us something contrary to what is revealed. But in things regarding which there is no revelation, it is by no means consistent with the character of a philosopher to accept as true what he has not ascertained to be such, and to trust more to the senses, in other words, to the inconsiderate judgments of childhood than to the dictates of mature reason.

---

[18] "reasonings."—FRENCH.

PART II.

OF THE PRINCIPLES OF MATERIAL THINGS.

I. The grounds on which the existence of material things may be known with certainty.

Although we are all sufficiently persuaded of the existence of material things, yet, since this was before called in question by us, and since we reckoned the persuasion of their existence as among the prejudices of our childhood, it is now necessary for us to investigate the grounds on which this truth may be known with certainty. In the first place, then, it cannot be doubted that every perception we have comes to us from some object different from our mind; for it is not in our power to cause ourselves to experience one perception rather than another, the perception being entirely dependent on the object which affects our senses. It may, indeed, be matter of inquiry whether that object be God, or something different from God; but because we perceive, or rather, stimulated by sense, clearly and distinctly apprehend, certain matter extended in length, breadth, and thickness, the various parts of which have different figures and motions, and give rise to the sensation we have of colours, smells, pain, etc., God would, without question, deserve to be regarded as a deceiver, if he directly and of himself presented to our mind the idea of this extended matter, or merely caused it to be presented to us by some object which possessed neither extension, figure, nor motion. For we clearly conceive this matter as entirely distinct from God, and from ourselves, or our mind; and appear even clearly to discern that the idea of it is formed in us on occasion of objects existing out of our minds, to which it is in every respect similar. But since God cannot deceive us, for this is repugnant to his nature, as has been already remarked, we must unhesitatingly conclude that there exists a certain object extended in length, breadth, and thickness, and possessing all those properties which we clearly apprehend to belong to what is extended. And this extended substance is what we call body or matter.

II. How we likewise know that the human body is closely connected with the mind.

We ought also to conclude that a certain body is more closely united to our mind than any other, because we clearly observe that pain and other sensations affect us without our foreseeing them; and these, the mind is conscious, do not arise from itself alone, nor pertain to it, in so far as it is a thing which thinks, but only in so far as it is united to another thing extended and movable, which is called the human body. But this is not the place to treat in detail of this matter.

III. That the perceptions of the senses do not teach us what is in reality in things, but what is beneficial of hurtful to the composite whole of mind and body.

It will be sufficient to remark that the perceptions of the senses are merely to be referred to this intimate union of the human body and mind, and that they usually make us aware of what, in external objects, may be useful or adverse to this union, but do not present to us these objects as they are in themselves, unless occasionally and by accident. For, after this observation, we will without difficulty lay aside the prejudices of the senses, and will have recourse to our understanding alone on this question by reflecting carefully on the ideas implanted in it by nature.

IV. That the nature of body consists not in weight hardness, colour and the like, but in extension alone.

In this way we will discern that the nature of matter or body, considered in general, does not consist in its being hard, or ponderous, or coloured, or that which affects our senses in any other way, but simply in its being a substance extended in length, breadth, and depth. For with respect to hardness, we know nothing of it by sense farther than that the parts of hard bodies resist the motion of our hands on coming into contact with them; but if every time our hands moved towards any part, all the bodies in that place receded as quickly as our hands approached, we should never feel hardness; and yet we have no reason to believe that bodies which might thus recede would on this account lose that which makes them bodies. The nature of body does not, therefore, consist in hardness. In the same way, it may be shown that weight, colour, and all the other qualities of this sort, which are perceived in corporeal matter, may be taken from it, itself meanwhile remaining entire: it thus follows that the nature of body depends on none of these.

V. That the truth regarding the nature of body is obscured by the opinions respecting rarefaction and a vacuum with which we are pre-occupied.

There still remain two causes to prevent its being fully admitted that the true nature of body consists in extension alone. The first is the prevalent opinion, that most bodies admit of being so rarefied and condensed that, when rarefied, they have greater extension than when condensed; and some even have subtilized to such a degree as to make a distinction between the substance of body and its quantity, and between quantity itself and extension. The second cause is this, that where we conceive only extension in length, breadth, and depth, we are not in the habit of saying that body is there, but only space and further void space, which the generality believe to be a mere negation.

VI. In what way rarefaction takes place.

But with regard to rarefaction and condensation, whoever gives his attention to his own thoughts, and admits nothing of which he is not clearly conscious, will not suppose that there is anything in those processes further than a change of figure in the body rarefied or condensed: so that, in other words, rare bodies are those between the parts of which there are numerous distances filled with other bodies; and dense bodies, on the other hand, those whose parts approaching each other, either diminish these distances or take them wholly away, in the latter of which cases the body is rendered absolutely dense. The body, however, when condensed, has not, therefore, less extension than when the parts embrace a greater space, owing to their removal from each other, and their dispersion into branches. For we ought not to attribute to it the extension of the pores or distances which its parts do not occupy when it is rarefied, but to the other bodies that fill these interstices; just as when we see a sponge full of water or any other liquid, we do not suppose that each part of the sponge has on this account greater extension than when compressed and dry, but only that its pores are wider, and therefore that the body is diffused over a larger space.

VII. That rarefaction cannot be intelligibly explained unless in the way here proposed.

And indeed I am unable to discover the force of the reasons which have induced some to say that rarefaction is the result of the augmentation of the quantity of body, rather than to explain it on the principle exemplified in the case of a sponge. For although when air or water is rarefied we do not see any of the pores that are rendered large, or the new body that is added to occupy them, it is yet less agreeable to reason to suppose something that is unintelligible for the purpose of giving a verbal and merely apparent explanation of the rarefaction of bodies, than to conclude, because of their rarefaction, that there are pores or distances between the parts which are increased in size, and filled with some new body. Nor ought we to refrain from assenting to this explanation, because we perceive this new body by none of our senses, for there is no reason which obliges us to believe that we should perceive by our senses all the bodies in existence. And we see that it is very easy to explain rarefaction in this manner, but impossible in any other; for, in fine, there would be, as appears to me, a manifest contradiction in supposing that any body was increased by a quantity or extension which it had not before, without the addition to it of a new extended substance, in other words, of another body, because it is impossible to conceive any addition of extension or quantity to a thing without supposing the addition of a substance having quantity or extension, as will more clearly appear from what follows.

VIII. That quantity and number differ only in thought (RATIONE) from that which has quantity and is numbered.

For quantity differs from extended substance, and number from what is numbered, not in reality but merely in our thought; so that, for example, we may consider the whole nature of a corporeal substance which is comprised in a space of ten feet, although we do not attend to this measure of ten feet, for the obvious reason that the thing conceived is of the same nature in any part of that space as in the whole; and, on the other hand, we can conceive the number ten, as also a continuous quantity of ten feet, without thinking of this determinate substance, because the concept of the number ten is manifestly the same whether we consider a number of ten feet or ten of anything else; and we can conceive a continuous quantity of ten feet without thinking of this or that determinate substance, although we cannot conceive it without some extended substance of which it is the quantity. It is in reality, however, impossible that any, even the least part, of such quantity or extension, can be taken away, without the retrenchment at the same time of as much of the substance, nor, on the other hand, can we lessen the substance, without at the same time taking as much from the quantity or extension.

IX. That corporeal substance, when distinguished from its quantity, is confusedly conceived as something incorporeal.

Although perhaps some express themselves otherwise on this matter, I am nevertheless convinced that they do not think differently from what I have now said: for when they distinguish (corporeal) substance from extension or quantity, they either mean nothing by the word (corporeal) substance, or they form in their minds merely a confused idea of incorporeal substance, which they falsely attribute to corporeal, and leave to extension the true idea of this corporeal substance; which extension they call an accident, but with such impropriety as to make it easy to discover that their words are not in harmony with their thoughts.

X. What space or internal place is.

Space or internal place, and the corporeal substance which is comprised in it, are not different in reality, but merely in the mode in which they are wont to be conceived by us. For, in truth, the same extension in length, breadth, and depth, which constitutes space, constitutes body; and the difference between them lies only in this, that in body we consider extension as particular, and conceive it to change with the body; whereas in space we attribute to extension a generic unity, so that after taking from a certain space the body which occupied it, we do not suppose that we have at the same time removed the extension of the space, because it appears to us that the same extension remains there so long as it is of the same magnitude and figure, and preserves the same situation in respect to certain bodies around it, by means of which we determine this space.

XI. How space is not in reality different from corporeal substance.

And indeed it will be easy to discern that it is the same extension which constitutes the nature of body as of space, and that these two things are mutually diverse only as the nature of the genus and species differs from that of the individual, provided we reflect on the idea we have of any body, taking a stone for example, and reject all that is not essential to the nature of body. In the first place, then, hardness may be rejected, because if the stone were liquefied or reduced to powder, it would no longer possess hardness, and yet would not cease to be a body; colour also may be thrown out of account, because we have frequently seen stones so transparent as to have no colour; again, we may reject weight, because we have the case of fire, which, though very light, is still a body; and, finally, we may reject cold, heat, and all the other qualities of this sort, either because they are not considered as in the stone, or because, with the change of these qualities, the stone is not supposed to have lost the nature of body. After this examination we will find that nothing remains in the idea of body, except that it is something extended in length, breadth, and depth; and this something is comprised in our idea of space, not only of that which is full of body, but even of what is called void space.

XII. How space differs from body in our mode of conceiving it.

There is, however, some difference between them in the mode of conception; for if we remove a stone from the space or place in which it was, we conceive that its extension also is taken away, because we regard this as particular, and inseparable from the stone itself: but meanwhile we suppose that the same extension of place in which this stone was remains, although the place of the stone be occupied by wood, water, air, or by any other body, or be even supposed vacant, because we now consider extension in general, and think that the same is common to stones, wood, water, air, and other bodies, and even to a vacuum itself, if there is any such thing, provided it be of the same magnitude and figure as before, and preserve the same situation among the external bodies which determine this space.

XIII. What external place is.

The reason of which is, that the words place and space signify nothing really different from body which is said to be in place, but merely designate its magnitude, figure, and situation among other bodies. For it is necessary, in order to determine this situation, to regard certain other bodies which we consider as immovable; and, according as we look to different bodies, we may see that the same thing at the same time does and does not change place. For example, when a vessel is being carried out to sea, a person sitting at the stern may be said to remain always in one place, if we look to the parts of the vessel, since with respect to these he preserves the same situation; and on the other hand, if regard be had to the neighbouring shores, the same person will seem to be perpetually changing place, seeing he is constantly receding from one shore and approaching another. And besides, if we suppose that the earth moves, and that it makes precisely as much way from west to east as the vessel from east to west, we will again say that the person at the stern does not change his place, because this place will be determined by certain immovable points which we imagine to be in the heavens. But if at length we are persuaded that there are no points really immovable in the universe, as will hereafter be shown to be probable, we will thence conclude that nothing has a permanent place unless in so far as it is fixed by our thought.

XIV. Wherein place and space differ.

The terms place and space, however, differ in signification, because place more expressly designates situation than magnitude or figure, while, on the other hand, we think of the latter when we speak of space. For we frequently say that a thing succeeds to the place of another, although it be not exactly of the same magnitude or figure; but we do not therefore admit that it occupies the same space as the other; and when the situation is changed we say that the place also is changed, although there are the same magnitude and figure as before: so that when we say that a thing is in a particular place, we mean merely that it is situated in a determinate way in respect of certain other objects; and when we add that it occupies such a space or place, we understand besides that it is of such determinate magnitude and figure as exactly to fill this space.

XV. How external place is rightly taken for the superficies of the surrounding body.

And thus we never indeed distinguish space from extension in length, breadth, and depth; we sometimes, however, consider place as in the thing placed, and at other times as out of it. Internal place indeed differs in no way from space; but external place may be taken for the superficies that immediately surrounds the thing placed. It ought to be remarked that by superficies we do not here understand any part of the surrounding body, but only the boundary between the surrounding and surrounded bodies, which is nothing more than a mode; or at least that we speak of superficies in general which is no part of one body rather than another, but is always considered the same, provided it retain the same magnitude and figure. For although the whole surrounding body with its superficies were changed, it would not be supposed that the body which was surrounded by it had therefore changed its place, if it meanwhile preserved the same situation with respect to the other bodies that are regarded as immovable. Thus, if we suppose that a boat is carried in one direction by the current of a stream, and impelled by the wind in the opposite with an equal force, so that its situation with respect to the banks is not changed, we will readily admit that it remains in the same place, although the whole superficies which surrounds it is incessantly changing.

XVI. That a vacuum or space in which there is absolutely no body is repugnant to reason.

With regard to a vacuum, in the philosophical sense of the term, that is, a space in which there is no substance, it is evident that such does not exist, seeing the extension of space or internal place is not different from that of body. For since from this alone, that a body has extension in length, breadth, and depth, we have reason to conclude that it is a substance, it being absolutely contradictory that nothing should possess extension, we ought to form a similar inference regarding the space which is supposed void, viz., that since there is extension in it there is necessarily also substance.

XVII. That a vacuum in the ordinary use of the term does not exclude all body.

And, in truth, by the term vacuum in its common use, we do not mean a place or space in which there is absolutely nothing, but only a place in which there is none of those things we presume ought to be there. Thus, because a pitcher is made to hold water, it is said to be empty when it is merely filled with air; or if there are no fish in a fish-pond, we say there is nothing in it, although it be full of water; thus a vessel is said to be empty, when, in place of the merchandise which it was designed to carry, it is loaded with sand only, to enable it to resist the violence of the wind; and, finally, it is in the same sense that we say space is void when it contains nothing sensible, although it contain created and self-subsisting matter; for we are not in the habit of considering the bodies near us, unless in so far as they cause in our organs of sense, impressions strong enough to enable us to perceive them. And if, in place of keeping in mind what ought to be understood by these terms a vacuum and nothing, we afterwards suppose that in the space we called a vacuum, there is not only no sensible object, but no object at all, we will fall into the same error as if, because a pitcher in which there is nothing but air, is, in common speech, said to be empty, we were therefore to judge that the air contained in it is not a substance (RES SUBSISTENS).

XVIII. How the prejudice of an absolute vacuum is to be corrected.

We have almost all fallen into this error from the earliest age, for, observing that there is no necessary connection between a vessel and the body it contains, we thought that God at least could take from a vessel the body which occupied it, without it being necessary that any other should be put in the place of the one removed. But that we may be able now to correct this false opinion, it is necessary to remark that there is in truth no connection between the vessel and the particular body which it contains, but that there is an absolutely necessary connection between the concave figure of the vessel and the extension considered generally which must be comprised in this cavity; so that it is not more contradictory to conceive a mountain without a valley than such a cavity without the extension it contains, or this extension apart from an extended substance, for, as we have often said, of nothing there can be no extension. And accordingly, if it be asked what would happen were God to remove from a vessel all the body contained in it, without permitting another body to occupy its place, the answer must be that the sides of the vessel would thus come into proximity with each other. For two bodies must touch each other when there is nothing between them, and it is manifestly contradictory for two bodies to be apart, in other words, that there should be a distance between them, and this distance yet be nothing; for all distance is a mode of extension, and cannot therefore exist without an extended substance.

XIX. That this confirms what was said of rarefaction.

After we have thus remarked that the nature of corporeal substance consists only in its being an extended thing, and that its extension is not different from that which we attribute to space, however empty, it is easy to discover the impossibility of any one of its parts in any way whatsoever occupying more space at one time than at another, and thus of being otherwise rarefied than in the way explained above; and it is easy to perceive also that there cannot be more matter or body in a vessel when it is filled with lead or gold, or any other body however heavy and hard, than when it but contains air and is supposed to be empty: for the quantity of the parts of which a body is composed does not depend on their weight or hardness, but only on the extension, which is always equal in the same vase.

XX. That from this the non-existence of atoms may likewise be demonstrated.

We likewise discover that there cannot exist any atoms or parts of matter that are of their own nature indivisible. For however small we suppose these parts to be, yet because they are necessarily extended, we are always able in thought to divide any one of them into two or more smaller parts, and may accordingly admit their divisibility. For there is nothing we can divide in thought which we do not thereby recognize to be divisible; and, therefore, were we to judge it indivisible our judgment would not be in harmony with the knowledge we have of the thing; and although we should even suppose that God had reduced any particle of matter to a smallness so extreme that it did not admit of being further divided, it would nevertheless be improperly styled indivisible, for though God had rendered the particle so small that it was not in the power of any creature to divide it, he could not however deprive himself of the ability to do so, since it is absolutely impossible for him to lessen his own omnipotence, as was before observed. Wherefore, absolutely speaking, the smallest extended particle is always divisible, since it is such of its very nature.

XXI. It is thus also demonstrated that the extension of the world is indefinite.

We further discover that this world or the whole (universitas) of corporeal substance, is extended without limit, for wherever we fix a limit, we still not only imagine beyond it spaces indefinitely extended, but perceive these to be truly imaginable, in other words, to be in reality such as we imagine them; so that they contain in them corporeal substance indefinitely extended, for, as has been already shown at length, the idea of extension which we conceive in any space whatever is plainly identical with the idea of corporeal substance.

XXII. It also follows that the matter of the heavens and earth is the same, and that there cannot be a plurality of worlds.

And it may also be easily inferred from all this that the earth and heavens are made of the same matter; and that even although there were an infinity of worlds, they would all be composed of this matter; from which it follows that a plurality of worlds is impossible, because we clearly conceive that the matter whose nature consists only in its being an extended substance, already wholly occupies all the imaginable spaces where these other worlds could alone be, and we cannot find in ourselves the idea of any other matter.

XXIII. That all the variety of matter, or the diversity of its forms, depends on motion.

There is therefore but one kind of matter in the whole universe, and this we know only by its being extended. All the properties we distinctly perceive to belong to it are reducible to its capacity of being divided and moved according to its parts; and accordingly it is capable of all those affections which we perceive can arise from the motion of its parts. For the partition of matter in thought makes no change in it; but all variation of it, or diversity of form, depends on motion. The philosophers even seem universally to have observed this, for they said that nature was the principle of motion and rest, and by nature they understood that by which all corporeal things become such as they are found in experience.

XXIV. What motion is, taking the term in its common use.

But motion (viz., local, for I can conceive no other kind of motion, and therefore I do not think we ought to suppose there is any other in nature), in the ordinary sense of the term, is nothing more than the action by which a body passes from one place to another. And just as we have remarked above that the same thing may be said to change and not to change place at the same time, so also we may say that the same thing is at the same time moved and not moved. Thus, for example, a person seated in a vessel which is setting sail, thinks he is in motion if he look to the shore that he has left, and consider it as fixed;

but not if he regard the ship itself, among the parts of which he preserves always the same situation. Moreover, because we are accustomed to suppose that there is no motion without action, and that in rest there is the cessation of action, the person thus seated is more properly said to be at rest than in motion, seeing he is not conscious of being in action.

XXV. What motion is properly so called.

But if, instead of occupying ourselves with that which has no foundation, unless in ordinary usage, we desire to know what ought to be understood by motion according to the truth of the thing, we may say, in order to give it a determinate nature, that it is THE TRANSPORTING OF ONE PART OF MATTER OR OF ONE BODY FROM THE VICINITY OF THOSE BODIES THAT ARE IN IMMEDIATE CONTACT WITH IT, OR WHICH WE REGARD AS AT REST, to the vicinity of other bodies. By a body as a part of matter, I understand all that which is transferred together, although it be perhaps composed of several parts, which in themselves have other motions; and I say that it is the transporting and not the force or action which transports, with the view of showing that motion is always in the movable thing, not in that which moves; for it seems to me that we are not accustomed to distinguish these two things with sufficient accuracy. Farther, I understand that it is a mode of the movable thing, and not a substance, just as figure is a property of the thing figured, and repose of that which is at rest.

PART III.

OF THE VISIBLE WORLD.

I. That we cannot think too highly of the works of God.

Having now ascertained certain principles of material things, which were sought, not by the prejudices of the senses, but by the light of reason, and which thus possess so great evidence that we cannot doubt of their truth, it remains for us to consider whether from these alone we can deduce the explication of all the phenomena of nature. We will commence with those phenomena that are of the greatest generality, and upon which the others depend, as, for example, with the general structure of this whole visible world. But in order to our philosophizing aright regarding this, two things are first of all to be observed. The first is, that we should ever bear in mind the infinity of the power and goodness of God, that we may not fear falling into error by imagining his works to be too great, beautiful, and perfect, but that we may, on the contrary, take care lest, by supposing limits to them of which we have no certain knowledge, we appear to think less highly than we ought of the power of God.

II. That we ought to beware lest, in our presumption, we imagine that the ends which God proposed to himself in the creation of the world are understood by us.

The second is, that we should beware of presuming too highly of ourselves, as it seems we should do if we supposed certain limits to the world, without being assured of their existence either by natural reasons or by divine revelation, as if the power of our thought extended beyond what God has in reality made; but likewise still more if we persuaded ourselves that all things were created by God for us only, or if we merely supposed that we could comprehend by the power of our intellect the ends which God proposed to himself in creating the universe.

III. In what sense it may be said that all things were created for the sake of man.

For although, as far as regards morals, it may be a pious thought to believe that God made all things for us, seeing we may thus be incited to greater gratitude and love toward him; and although it is even in some sense true, because there is no created thing of which we cannot make some use, if it be only that of exercising our mind in considering it, and honouring God on account of it, it is yet by no means probable that all things were created for us in this way that God had no other end in their creation; and this supposition would be plainly ridiculous and inept in physical reasoning, for we do not doubt but that many things exist, or formerly existed and have now ceased to be, which were never seen or known by man, and were never of use to him.

PART IV.

OF THE EARTH.

CLXXXVIII. Of what is to be borrowed from disquisitions on animals and man to advance the knowledge of material objects.

I should add nothing farther to this the Fourth Part of the Principles of Philosophy, did I purpose carrying out my original design of writing a Fifth and Sixth Part, the one treating of things possessed of life, that is, animals and plants, and the other of man. But because I have not yet acquired sufficient knowledge of all the matters of which I should desire to treat in these two last parts, and do not know whether I shall ever have sufficient leisure to finish them, I will here subjoin a few things regarding the objects of our senses, that I may not, for the sake of the latter, delay too long the publication of the former parts, or of what may be desiderated in them, which I might have reserved for explanation in those others: for I have hitherto described this earth, and generally the whole visible world, as if it were merely a machine in which there was nothing at all to consider except the figures and motions of its parts, whereas our senses present to us many other things, for example colours, smells, sounds, and the like, of which, if I did not speak at all, it would be thought I had omitted the explication of the majority of the objects that are in nature.

CLXXXIX. What perception (SENSUS) is, and how we perceive.

We must know, therefore, that although the human soul is united to the whole body, it has, nevertheless, its principal seat in the brain, where alone it not only understands and imagines, but also perceives; and this by the medium of the nerves, which are extended like threads from the brain to all the other members, with which they are so connected that we can hardly touch any one of them without moving the extremities of some of the nerves spread over it; and this motion passes to the other extremities of those nerves which are collected in the brain round the seat of the soul, as I have already explained with sufficient minuteness in the fourth chapter of the Dioptrics. But the movements which are thus excited in the brain by the nerves variously affect the soul or mind, which is intimately conjoined with the brain, according to the diversity of the motions themselves. And the diverse affections of the mind or thoughts that immediately arise from these motions, are called perceptions of the senses (SENSUUM PERCEPTIONES), or, as we commonly speak, sensations (SENSUS).

CXC. Of the distinction of the senses; and, first, of the internal, that is, of the affections of the mind (passions), and the natural appetites.

The varieties of these sensations depend, firstly, on the diversity of the nerves themselves, and, secondly, of the movements that are made in each nerve. We have not, however, as many different senses as there are nerves. We can distinguish but seven principal classes of nerves, of which two belong to the internal, and the other five to the external senses. The nerves which extend to the stomach, the oesophagus, the fauces, and the other internal parts that are subservient to our natural wants, constitute one of our internal senses. This is called the natural appetite (APPETITUS NATURALIS). The other internal sense, which embraces all the emotions (COMMOTIONES) of the mind or passions, and affections, as joy, sadness, love, hate, and the like, depends upon the nerves which extend to the heart and the parts about the heart, and are exceedingly small; for, by way of example, when the blood happens to be pure and well tempered, so that it dilates in the heart more readily and strongly than usual, this so enlarges and moves the small nerves scattered around the orifices, that there is thence a corresponding movement in the brain, which affects the mind with a certain natural feeling of joy; and as often as these same nerves are moved in the same way, although this is by other causes, they excite in our mind the same feeling (sensus, sentiment). Thus, the imagination of the enjoyment of a good does not contain in itself the feeling of joy, but it causes the animal spirits to pass from the brain to the muscles in which these nerves are inserted; and thus dilating the orifices of the heart, it also causes these small nerves to move in the way appointed by nature to afford the sensation of joy. Thus, when we receive news, the mind first of all judges of it, and if the news be good, it rejoices with that intellectual joy (GAUDIUM INTELLECTUALE) which is independent of any emotion (COMMOTIO) of the body, and which the Stoics did not deny to their wise man [although they supposed him exempt from all passion]. But as soon as this joy passes from the understanding to the imagination, the spirits flow from the brain to the muscles that are about the heart, and there excite the motion of the small nerves, by means of which another motion is caused in the brain, which affects the mind with the sensation of animal joy (LAETITIA ANIMALIS). On the same principle, when the blood is so thick that it flows but sparingly into the ventricles of the heart, and is not there sufficiently dilated, it excites in the same nerves a motion quite different from the preceding, which, communicated to the brain, gives to the mind the sensation of sadness, although the mind itself is perhaps ignorant of the cause of its sadness. And all the other causes which move these nerves in the same way may also give to the mind the same sensation. But the other movements of the same nerves produce other effects, as the feelings of love, hate, fear, anger, etc., as far as they are merely affections or passions of the mind; in other words, as far as they are confused thoughts which the mind has not from itself alone, but from its being closely joined to the body, from which it receives impressions; for there is the widest difference between these passions and the distinct thoughts which we have of what ought to be loved, or chosen, or shunned, etc., [although these are often enough found together]. The natural appetites, as

60

hunger, thirst, and the others, are likewise sensations excited in the mind by means of the nerves of the stomach, fauces, and other parts, and are entirely different from the will which we have to eat, drink, [and to do all that which we think proper for the conservation of our body]; but, because this will or appetition almost always accompanies them, they are therefore named appetites.

CXCI. Of the external senses; and first of touch.

We commonly reckon the external senses five in number, because there are as many different kinds of objects which move the nerves and their organs, and an equal number of kinds of confused thoughts excited in the soul by these emotions. In the first place, the nerves terminating in the skin of the whole body can be touched through this medium by any terrene objects whatever, and moved by these wholes, in one way by their hardness, in another by their gravity, in a third by their heat, in a fourth by their humidity, etc.--and in as many diverse modes as they are either moved or hindered from their ordinary motion, to that extent are diverse sensations excited in the mind, from which a corresponding number of tactile qualities derive their appellations. Besides this, when these nerves are moved a little more powerfully than usual, but not nevertheless to the degree by which our body is in any way hurt, there thus arises a sensation of titillation, which is naturally agreeable to the mind, because it testifies to it of the powers of the body with which it is joined, [in that the latter can suffer the action causing this titillation, without being hurt]. But if this action be strong enough to hurt our body in any way, this gives to our mind the sensation of pain. And we thus see why corporeal pleasure and pain, although sensations of quite an opposite character, arise nevertheless from causes nearly alike.

CXCII. Of taste.

In the second place, the other nerves scattered over the tongue and the parts in its vicinity are diversely moved by the particles of the same bodies, separated from each other and floating in the saliva in the mouth, and thus cause sensations of diverse tastes according to the diversity of figure in these particles.[19]

CXCIII. Of smell.

Thirdly, two nerves also or appendages of the brain, for they do not go beyond the limits of the skull, are moved by the particles of terrestrial bodies, separated and flying in the air, not indeed by all particles indifferently, but by those only that are sufficiently subtle and penetrating to enter the pores of the bone we call the spongy, when drawn into the nostrils, and thus to reach the nerves. From the different motions of these particles arise the sensations of the different smells.

------

[19] In the French this section begins, "Taste, after touch the grossest of the senses," etc.

CXCIV. Of hearing.

Fourthly, there are two nerves within the ears, so attached to three small bones that are mutually sustaining, and the first of which rests on the small membrane that covers the cavity we call the tympanum of the ear, that all the diverse vibrations which the surrounding air communicates to this membrane are transmitted to the mind by these nerves, and these vibrations give rise, according to their diversity, to the sensations of the different sounds.

CXCV. Of sight.

Finally, the extremities of the optic nerves, composing the coat in the eyes called the retina, are not moved by the air nor by any terrestrial object, but only by the globules of the second element, whence we have the sense of light and colours: as I have already at sufficient length explained in the Dioptrics and treatise of Meteors.[20]

CXCVI. That the soul perceives only in so far as it is in the brain.

It is clearly established, however, that the soul does not perceive in so far as it is in each member of the body, but only in so far as it is in the brain, where the nerves by their movements convey to it the diverse actions of the external objects that touch the parts of the body in which they are inserted. For, in the first place, there are various maladies, which, though they affect the brain alone, yet bring disorder upon, or deprive us altogether of the use of, our senses, just as sleep, which affects the brain only, and yet takes from us daily during a great part of our time the faculty of perception, which afterwards in our waking state is restored to us. The second proof is, that though there be no disease in the brain, [or in the members in which the organs of the external senses are], it is nevertheless sufficient to take away sensation from the part of the body where the nerves terminate, if only the movement of one of the nerves that extend from the brain to these members be obstructed in any part of the distance that is between the two. And the last proof is, that we sometimes feel pain as if in certain of our members, the cause of which, however, is not in these members where it is felt, but somewhere nearer the brain, through which the nerves pass that give to the mind the sensation of it. I could establish this fact by innumerable experiments; I will here, however, merely refer to one of them. A girl suffering from a bad ulcer in the hand, had her eyes bandaged whenever the surgeon came to visit her, not being able to bear the sight of the dressing of the sore; and, the gangrene having spread, after the expiry of a few days the arm was amputated from the elbow [without the girl's knowledge]; linen cloths tied one above the other were substituted in place of the part amputated, so that she remained for some time without knowing that the operation had been

---

[20] In the French this section begins, "Finally, sight is the most subtle of all the senses," etc.

performed, and meanwhile she complained of feeling various pains, sometimes in one finger of the hand that was cut off, and sometimes in another. The only explanation of this is, that the nerves which before stretched downwards from the brain to the hand, and then terminated in the arm close to the elbow, were there moved in the same way as they required to be moved before in the hand for the purpose of impressing on the mind residing in the brain the sensation of pain in this or that finger. [And this clearly shows that the pain of the hand is not felt by the mind in so far as it is in the hand, but in so far as it is in the brain.]

CXCVII. That the nature of the mind is such that from the motion alone of body the various sensations can be excited in it.

In the next place, it can be proved that our mind is of such a nature that the motions of the body alone are sufficient to excite in it all sorts of thoughts, without it being necessary that these should in any way resemble the motions which give rise to them, and especially that these motions can excite in it those confused thoughts called sensations (SENSUS, SENSATIONES). For we see that words, whether uttered by the voice or merely written, excite in our minds all kinds of thoughts and emotions. On the same paper, with the same pen and ink, by merely moving the point of the pen over the paper in a particular way, we can trace letters that will raise in the minds of our readers the thoughts of combats, tempests, or the furies, and the passions of indignation and sorrow; in place of which, if the pen be moved in another way hardly different from the former, this slight change will cause thoughts widely different from the above, such as those of repose, peace, pleasantness, and the quite opposite passions of love and joy. Some one will perhaps object that writing and speech do not immediately excite in the mind any passions, or imaginations of things different from the letters and sounds, but afford simply the knowledge of these, on occasion of which the mind, understanding the signification of the words, afterwards excites in itself the imaginations and passions that correspond to the words. But what will be said of the sensations of pain and titillation? The motion merely of a sword cutting a part of our skin causes pain, [but does not on that account make us aware of the motion or figure of the sword]. And it is certain that this sensation of pain is not less different from the motion that causes it, or from that of the part of our body which the sword cuts, than are the sensations we have of colour, sound, odour, or taste. On this ground we may conclude that our mind is of such a nature that the motions alone of certain bodies can also easily excite in it all the other sensations, as the motion of a sword excites in it the sensation of pain.

CXCVIII. That by our senses we know nothing of external objects beyond their figure [or situation], magnitude, and motion.

Besides, we observe no such difference between the nerves as to lead us to judge that one set of them convey to the brain from the organs of the external senses anything different from another, or that anything at

63

all reaches the brain besides the local motion of the nerves themselves. And we see that local motion alone causes in us not only the sensation of titillation and of pain, but also of light and sounds. For if we receive a blow on the eye of sufficient force to cause the vibration of the stroke to reach the retina, we see numerous sparks of fire, which, nevertheless, are not out of our eye; and when we stop our ear with our finger, we hear a humming sound, the cause of which can only proceed from the agitation of the air that is shut up within it. Finally, we frequently observe that heat [hardness, weight], and the other sensible qualities, as far as they are in objects, and also the forms of those bodies that are purely material, as, for example, the forms of fire, are produced in them by the motion of certain other bodies, and that these in their turn likewise produce other motions in other bodies. And we can easily conceive how the motion of one body may be caused by that of another, and diversified by the size, figure, and situation of its parts, but we are wholly unable to conceive how these same things (viz., size, figure, and motion), can produce something else of a nature entirely different from themselves, as, for example, those substantial forms and real qualities which many philosophers suppose to be in bodies; nor likewise can we conceive how these qualities or forms possess force to cause motions in other bodies. But since we know, from the nature of our soul, that the diverse motions of body are sufficient to produce in it all the sensations which it has, and since we learn from experience that several of its sensations are in reality caused by such motions, while we do not discover that anything besides these motions ever passes from the organs of the external senses to the brain, we have reason to conclude that we in no way likewise apprehend that in external objects, which we call light, colour, smell, taste, sound, heat or cold, and the other tactile qualities, or that which we call their substantial forms, unless as the various dispositions of these objects which have the power of moving our nerves in various ways.[21]

CXCIX. That there is no phenomenon of nature whose explanation has been omitted in this treatise.

And thus it may be gathered, from an enumeration that is easily made, that there is no phenomenon of nature whose explanation has been omitted in this treatise; for beyond what is perceived by the senses, there is nothing that can be considered a phenomenon of nature. But leaving out of account motion, magnitude, figure, [and the situation of the parts of each body], which I have explained as they exist in body, we perceive nothing out of us by our senses except light, colours, smells, tastes, sounds, and the tactile qualities; and these I have recently shown to be nothing more, at least so far as they are known to us, than certain dispositions of the objects, consisting in magnitude, figure, and motion.

---

[21] "the diverse figures, situations, magnitudes, and motions of their parts."-- French.

CC. That this treatise contains no principles which are not universally received; and that this philosophy is not new, but of all others the most ancient and common.

But I am desirous also that it should be observed that, though I have here endeavoured to give an explanation of the whole nature of material things, I have nevertheless made use of no principle which was not received and approved by Aristotle, and by the other philosophers of all ages; so that this philosophy, so far from being new, is of all others the most ancient and common: for I have in truth merely considered the figure, motion, and magnitude of bodies, and examined what must follow from their mutual concourse on the principles of mechanics, which are confirmed by certain and daily experience. But no one ever doubted that bodies are moved, and that they are of various sizes and figures, according to the diversity of which their motions also vary, and that from mutual collision those somewhat greater than others are divided into many smaller, and thus change figure. We have experience of the truth of this, not merely by a single sense, but by several, as touch, sight, and hearing: we also distinctly imagine and understand it. This cannot be said of any of the other things that fall under our senses, as colours, sounds, and the like; for each of these affects but one of our senses, and merely impresses upon our imagination a confused image of itself, affording our understanding no distinct knowledge of what it is.

CCI. That sensible bodies are composed of insensible particles.

But I allow many particles in each body that are perceived by none of our senses, and this will not perhaps be approved of by those who take the senses for the measure of the knowable. [We greatly wrong human reason, however, as appears to me, if we suppose that it does not go beyond the eye-sight]; for no one can doubt that there are bodies so small as not to be perceptible by any of our senses, provided he only consider what is each moment added to those bodies that are being increased little by little, and what is taken from those that are diminished in the same way. A tree increases daily, and it is impossible to conceive how it becomes greater than it was before, unless we at the same time conceive that some body is added to it. But who ever observed by the senses those small bodies that are in one day added to a tree while growing? Among the philosophers at least, those who hold that quantity is indefinitely divisible, ought to admit that in the division the parts may become so small as to be wholly imperceptible. And indeed it ought not to be a matter of surprise, that we are unable to perceive very minute bodies; for the nerves that must be moved by objects to cause perception are not themselves very minute, but are like small cords, being composed of a quantity of smaller fibres, and thus the most minute bodies are not capable of moving them. Nor do I think that any one who makes use of his reason will deny that we philosophize with much greater truth when we judge of what takes place in those small bodies which are imperceptible from their minuteness only, after the analogy of what we see occurring in those we do perceive, [and in this way explain all that is in nature, as I have essayed to do in this treatise], than when we give an explanation of the same things by inventing I know not what novelties, that have no relation to the things we actually perceive, [as first matter, substantial forms, and all that grand array of qualities which many are in the habit of supposing, each of which is more difficult to comprehend than all that is professed to be explained by means of them].

CCII. That the philosophy of Democritus is not less different from ours than from the common. [22]

But it may be said that Democritus also supposed certain corpuscles that were of various figures, sizes, and motions, from the heaping together and mutual concourse of which all sensible bodies arose; and, nevertheless, his mode of philosophizing is commonly rejected by all. To this I reply that the philosophy of Democritus was never rejected by any one, because he allowed the existence of bodies smaller than those we perceive, and attributed to them diverse sizes, figures, and motions, for no one can doubt that there are in reality such, as we have already shown; but it was rejected, in the first place, because he supposed that these corpuscles were indivisible, on which ground I also reject it; in the second place, because he imagined there was a vacuum about them, which I show to be impossible; thirdly, because he attributed gravity to these bodies, of which I deny the existence in any body, in so far as a body is considered by itself, because it is a quality that depends on the relations of situation and motion which several bodies bear to each other; and, finally, because he has not explained in particular how all things arose from the concourse of corpuscles alone, or, if he gave this explanation with regard to a few of them, his whole reasoning was far from being coherent, [or such as would warrant us in extending the same explanation to the whole of nature]. This, at least, is the verdict we must give regarding his philosophy, if we may judge of his opinions from what has been handed down to us in writing. I leave it to others to determine whether the philosophy I profess possesses a valid coherency, [and whether on its principles we can make the requisite number of deductions; and, inasmuch as the consideration of figure, magnitude, and motion has been admitted by Aristotle and by all the others, as well as by Democritus, and since I reject all that the latter has supposed, with this single exception, while I reject generally all that has been supposed by the others, it is plain that this mode of philosophizing has no more affinity with that of Democritus than of any other particular sect].

CCIII. How we may arrive at the knowledge of the figures, [magnitudes], and motions of the insensible particles of bodies.

---

[22] "that of Aristotle or the others."--French.

But, since I assign determinate figures, magnitudes, and motions to the insensible particles of bodies, as if I had seen them, whereas I admit that they do not fall under the senses, some one will perhaps demand how I have come by my knowledge of them. [To this I reply, that I first considered in general all the clear and distinct notions of material things that are to be found in our understanding, and that, finding no others except those of figures, magnitudes, and motions, and of the rules according to which these three things can be diversified by each other, which rules are the principles of geometry and mechanics, I judged that all the knowledge man can have of nature must of necessity be drawn from this source; because all the other notions we have of sensible things, as confused and obscure, can be of no avail in affording us the knowledge of anything out of ourselves, but must serve rather to impede it]. Thereupon, taking as my ground of inference the simplest and best known of the principles that have been implanted in our minds by nature, I considered the chief differences that could possibly subsist between the magnitudes, and figures, and situations of bodies insensible on account of their smallness alone, and what sensible effects could be produced by their various modes of coming into contact; and afterwards, when I found like effects in the bodies that we perceive by our senses, I judged that they could have been thus produced, especially since no other mode of explaining them could be devised. And in this matter the example of several bodies made by art was of great service to me: for I recognize no difference between these and natural bodies beyond this, that the effects of machines depend for the most part on the agency of certain instruments, which, as they must bear some proportion to the hands of those who make them, are always so large that their figures and motions can be seen; in place of which, the effects of natural bodies almost always depend upon certain organs so minute as to escape our senses. And it is certain that all the rules of mechanics belong also to physics, of which it is a part or species, [so that all that is artificial is withal natural]: for it is not less natural for a clock, made of the requisite number of wheels, to mark the hours, than for a tree, which has sprung from this or that seed, to produce the fruit peculiar to it. Accordingly, just as those who are familiar with automata, when they are informed of the use of a machine, and see some of its parts, easily infer from these the way in which the others, that are not seen by them, are made; so from considering the sensible effects and parts of natural bodies, I have essayed to determine the character of their causes and insensible parts.

CCIV. That, touching the things which our senses do not perceive, it is sufficient to explain how they can be, [and that this is all that Aristotle has essayed].

But here some one will perhaps reply, that although I have supposed causes which could produce all natural objects, we ought not on this account to conclude that they were produced by these causes; for, just as the same artisan can make two clocks, which, though they both equally well indicate the time, and are not different in outward appearance, have nevertheless nothing resembling in the composition of their wheels; so doubtless the Supreme Maker of things has an infinity of diverse means at his disposal, by each of which he could have made all the things of this world to appear as we see them, without it being possible for the human mind to know which of all these means he chose to employ. I most freely concede this; and I believe that I have done all that was required, if the causes I have assigned are such that their effects accurately correspond to all the phenomena of nature, without determining whether it is by these or by others that they are actually produced. And it will be sufficient for the use of life to know the causes thus imagined, for medicine, mechanics, and in general all the arts to which the knowledge of physics is of service, have for their end only those effects that are sensible, and that are accordingly to be reckoned among the phenomena of nature.[23]

And lest it should be supposed that Aristotle did, or professed to do, anything more than this, it ought to be remembered that he himself expressly says, at the commencement of the seventh chapter of the first book of the Meteorologies, that, with regard to things which are not manifest to the senses, he thinks to adduce sufficient reasons and demonstrations of them, if he only shows that they may be such as he explains them.[24]

CCV. That nevertheless there is a moral certainty that all the things of this world are such as has been here shown they may be.

But nevertheless, that I may not wrong the truth by supposing it less certain than it is, I will here distinguish two kinds of certitude. The first is called moral, that is, a certainty sufficient for the conduct of life, though, if we look to the absolute power of God, what is morally certain may be false. [Thus, those who never visited Rome do not doubt that it is a city of Italy, though it might be that all from whom they got their information were deceived]. Again, if any one, wishing to decipher a letter written in Latin characters that are not placed in regular order, bethinks himself of reading a B wherever an A is found, and a C wherever there is a B, and thus of substituting in place of each letter the one which follows it in the order of the alphabet, and if by this means he finds that there are certain Latin words composed of these, he will not doubt that the true meaning of the writing is contained in these words, although he may discover this only by conjecture, and although it is possible that the writer of it did not arrange the letters on this principle of alphabetical order, but on some other, and thus concealed another meaning in it: for this is so improbable [especially when the cipher

---

[23] "have for their end only to apply certain sensible bodies to each other in such a way that, in the course of natural causes, certain sensible effects may be produced; and we will be able to accomplish this quite as well by considering the series of certain causes thus imagined, although false, as if they were the true, since this series is supposed similar as far as regards sensible effects."-French.

[24] words in Greek

contains a number of words] as to seem incredible. But they who observe how many things regarding the magnet, fire, and the fabric of the whole world, are here deduced from a very small number of principles, though they deemed that I had taken them up at random and without grounds, will yet perhaps acknowledge that it could hardly happen that so many things should cohere if these principles were false.

CCVI. That we possess even more than a moral certainty of it.

Besides, there are some, even among natural, things which we judge to be absolutely certain. [Absolute certainty arises when we judge that it is impossible a thing can be otherwise than as we think it]. This certainty is founded on the metaphysical ground, that, as God is supremely good and the source of all truth, the faculty of distinguishing truth from error which he gave us, cannot be fallacious so long as we use it aright, and distinctly perceive anything by it. Of this character are the demonstrations of mathematics, the knowledge that material things exist, and the clear reasonings that are formed regarding them. The results I have given in this treatise will perhaps be admitted to a place in the class of truths that are absolutely certain, if it be considered that they are deduced in a continuous series from the first and most elementary principles of human knowledge; especially if it be sufficiently understood that we can perceive no external objects unless some local motion be caused by them in our nerves, and that such motion cannot be caused by the fixed stars, owing to their great distance from us, unless a motion be also produced in them and in the whole heavens lying between them and us: for these points being admitted, all the others, at least the more general doctrines which I have advanced regarding the world or earth [e. g., the fluidity of the heavens, Part III., Section XLVI.], will appear to be almost the only possible explanations of the phenomena they present.

CCVII. That, however, I submit all my opinions to the authority of the church.

Nevertheless, lest I should presume too far, I affirm nothing, but submit all these my opinions to the authority of the church and the judgment of the more sage; and I desire no one to believe anything I may have said, unless he is constrained to admit it by the force and evidence of reason.

Printed in the United States
125889LV00011B/131/P

9 781595 476869